How to Start & Manage a Home Based Business

*A Practical Way to Start
Your Own Business*

By

Jerre G. Lewis and Leslie D. Renn

How To Start & Manage A Home-Based Business

ISBN 1-887005-11-0

Library of Congress Catalog Card Number
95-95310

Lewis & Renn Associates, Inc.   517-684-1184

To my wife Victoria, and my children Elizabeth, Marie, John, and Becky Lewis.

To my wife Donna, and my children Leslie, Kevin, Jeffrey, and Christine Renn.

TABLE OF CONTENTS

Chapter 1 - Introduction 1

Chapter 2 - Planning the Business 6

Chapter 3 - Marketing Strategies for Home-Based Business 11

Chapter 4 - Promoting the Home-Based Business 19

Chapter 5 - Financial Planning for Home-Based Businesses 24

Chapter 6 - Home-Based Business Planning 33

Chapter 7 - Managing the Home-Based Business 57

Chapter 8 - Franchise Outline 60

Chapter 9 - Home-Based Business Resources 66

Chapter 10 - Home-Based Small Business Computer Information 80

Appendix A - A Concise Guide to Starting Your Own Business ....

Appendix B - Business Forms ....

Appendix C - Business Plans Outline ....

Appendix D - Business Insurance Checklist ....

Chapter 1

Introduction

Selecting the right home based business opportunity requires careful, thorough evaluations of yourself, the type of business you would like to operate in your desired area, and those businesses that meet your needs and expectations. Owning your own business is as much a part of the American dream as owning a home, and for you, this urge represents one of life's most exciting challenges. This book is for those men and women who someday may go into business for themselves and for those who are already in business for themselves but wish to strengthen their entrepreneurial and managerial skills.

Entrepreneurs come in all shapes and sizes, personalities, and lifestyles. They are usually highly motivated, hard-working individuals who receive satisfaction from taking risks. Your business should interest you, not just be an income generator. Analyze your personal style. Do you like working with people? Are you a self starter, goal oriented, persistent, a risk taker, willing to work hard and long hours?

If you have been honest in evaluating yourself, you will now select the right type of business. Before you can determine which of the multitude of businesses is right for you to start, you must evaluate the businesses you want to start by asking these questions. Is the business area growing? How does the economy affect it? Who dominates its market? Once you have considered a business that satisfies your needs and interest you must prepare a formal business plan by following the outline given in this book.

Small businesses constitute a dynamic and critical sector of the U.S. economy. Every year in the United States more than 600,000 new businesses are launched by independent men and women eager to make their own decisions, express their own ideas, and be their own bosses. But running your own business is not as easy as it may seem. There can be problems with the inventory, or getting the right goods delivered on time. Yet, managing one's own business can be a personally and financially rewarding experience for an individual strong enough to meet the test. A person with stamina, maturity, and creativity, one who is willing to make sacrifices, may find making a go of a struggling enterprise an exhilarating challenge with many compensations.

Small business owners are a dedicated group of people who work hard and whose hours on the job usually exceed the nine-to-five routine. The owner's commitment is the key to many successful small businesses; an entrepreneur is able to communicate ideas, lead, plan, be patient, and word well with people.

Managing a business requires more than the possession of technical knowledge. Because most small businesses are started by technical people, such as engineers and salesmen, their managerial acumen is often less developed than their technical skills. The need to plan for management is common to every type of and size of business, and there are certain steps that must be taken. Although some of them are very elementary - such as applying for a city business permit - the most important are often complex and difficult and require the advice of specialists: accountants, attorneys, insurance brokers, and/or bankers. For almost any business though, the first step will be to translate the entrepreneur's basic idea into a concrete plan for action.

To gauge your level of entrepreneurial spirit, the following quiz was created. Please answer each question honestly and then total the columns.

ENTREPRENEURIAL QUIZ

	YES	NO	SOMETIMES
1. I am a self-starter. Nobody has to tell me how to get going.			
2. I am capable of getting along with just about everybody.			
3. I have no trouble getting people to follow my lead.			
4. I like to be in charge of things and see them through.			
5. I always plan ahead before beginning a project. I am usually the one who gets everyone organized.			
6. I have a lot of stamina. I can keep going as long as necessary.			
7. I have no trouble making decisions and can make up my mind in a hurry.			
8. I say exactly what I mean. People can trust me.			
9. Once I make my mind up to do something, nothing can stop me.			
10. I am in excellent health and have a lot of energy.			

	YES	NO	SOMETIMES

11. I have experience or technical knowledge in the business I intend to start.

12. I feel comfortable taking risks if it is something I really believe in.

13. I have good communication skills.

14. I am flexible in my dealings with people and situations.

15. I consider myself creative and resourceful.

16. I can analyze a situation and take steps to correct problems.

17. I think I am capable of maintaining a good working relationship with employees.

18. I am not a dictator. I am willing to listen to employees, customers and suppliers.

19. I am not rigid in my policies. I am willing to adjust to meet the needs of employees, customers, and suppliers.

20. More than anything else, I want to run my own business.

Total of Column #1 _____
Total of Column #2 _____
Total of Column #3 _____

If the total of Column #1 is the highest, then you will probably be very successful in running your own business.

If the total of Column #2 is the highest, you may find that running a business is more than you can handle.

If the total of Column #3 is the highest, you should consider taking on a partner who is strong in your weak areas.

NOTE: This quiz was adapted from the Small Business Administration publication "Checklist for Going into Business."

Chapter 2

Planning the Business

Technological innovations, changing attitudes and high business start-up costs have brought businesses - millions of businesses - homes The Small Business Administration estimates that about 29 million Americans run full or part-time businesses from their homes in 1994. There's no place like home to start a successful small business. The Dream of self-employment can be fulfilled. You don't need to finance the opening of an elaborate office or facility to start your own one-person corporation either. You can start your own home-based business.

Anyone preparing to run a home-based business needs to learn a great deal to assure the best possible chance for success.

GETTING STARTED

You will need to study yourself, your product or service, and sources of home-based information. The following is a list of what you need to accomplish to insure that your home-based endeavor will head in the right direction.

1. Define your educational background and work experience.

2. Survey all the basic types of home-based businesses.

3. Define what type of home-based business matched your experience and educational background.

6

4. Choose only the home-based business that you would like to own and operate.

5. Define what products or services your home-based business will be marketing.

6. Define who will be using your products/services.

7. Define why they will be purchasing your products/services.

8. List all competitions in your home-based marketing area.

ZONING REGISTRATION

Home-based businesses are subject to many laws and regulations enforced by state, county, township governmental units. Most jurisdictions now have codes, a zoning board, and an appeal board which regulate home businesses. Areas often are zoned residential, commercial or industrial.

You must become familiar with these regulations. If you are doing business in violation of these regulations, you could be issued a cease and desist order or fined.

Certain kinds of goods cannot be produced in the home, though these restrictions vary somewhat from state-to-state. Most states outlaws home production of fireworks, drugs, poisons, explosives, sanitary/medical product, and some toys.

Many localities have registration requirements for new businesses. You will need to obtain a work certificate or license from the state.

TAX REQUIREMENTS

Application for Employer Identification Number, Form SS-4. This registers you with the Internal Revenue Service as a business. If you have employees, you should ask for Circular E along with you ID number. Circular E explains federal income and social security tax withholding requirements.

Employer's Annual Unemployment Tax Return, Form 940. This is only if you have employees. It's used to report and pay the Federal Unemployment compensation Tax.

Employee's Withholding Allowance Certificate, W-4. Every employee must complete the W-r so the proper amount of income tax can be withheld from the employee's pay. If the employee claims more than 15 allowances or a complete withholding exemption while having a salary of more than $200 a week, a copy of the W-4 must go to the IRS.

Employer's Wage and Tax Statement, W-2. Used to report to the IRS the total taxes withheld and total compensation paid to each employee per year.

Reconciliation/Transmittal of Income and Tax Statements, W-3. Used to total all information from the W-2. Sent to the Social Security Administration.

The IRS puts on monthly workshops on understanding and using these forms. Call your local IRS office for further information.

States also have various tax form requirements including: an unemployment tax form, a certificate of registration application, a sales and use tax return, an employer's quarterly contribution and payroll report, an income tax withholding registration form, an income tax withholding form, and others. Some forms apply only to employers who have employees. Your local IRS office and state Office of Taxation can provide you with listings of forms you will need to start you business. The following table outlines Federal tax form requirements.

Every home-based business begins with an idea - a product to be manufactured or sold, a service to be performed.

Whatever the home-based business or its degree of complexity, the owner needs a business plan in order to transform a vision into a working operation.

This business plan should describe in writing and in figures the proposed home-based business and its products, services, or manufacturing processes. It should also include an analysis of the market, a marketing strategy, an organizational plan, and measurable financial objectives.

WHAT SHOULD A BUSINESS PLAN COVER?

It should be a thorough and objective analysis of both personal abilities and business requirements for a particular product or service. It should define strategies for such functions as marketing and production, organization and legal aspects, accounting and finance. A business plan should answer such questions as:

What do I want and what am I capable of doing?
What are the most workable ways of achieving my goals?
What can I expect in the future?

There is no single best way to begin. What follows is simply a guide and can be changed to suit individual needs.

1. Define long-term goals.
2. State short-term.
3. Set marketing strategies to meet goals and objectives.
4. Analyze available resources.
5. Assemble financial data.
6. Review plan.

Please refer to Figure 2.1 for a complete business plan outline.

9

The business operator with a realistic plan has the best chance for success.

Figure 2.1

BUSINESS PLAN FOR SMALL BUSINESSES

I.   Type of Business

II. Location

III. Target Market

IV. Planning Process

V.   Organizational Structure

VI. Staffing Procedures

VII. Market Strategy

IX. Financial Planning

X.   Budgeted Balance Sheet

XI. Budgeted Income Statement

XII. Budgeted Cash Flow Statement

XIII. Break-Even Chart

CHAPTER 3

Marketing Strategies
for Home-Based Businesses

As a potential home-based business owner, it is important to learn all you can about marketing. You will need to know how to identify your market and how to market your product or service.

As a business person who looks for a profit from the sale of goods, you recognize that without people who want to buy, there is no demand for the things you want to sell. Thus, it is important that, in addition to knowing about the functions of marketing, you also study the activities that will influence the consumer. When you satisfy the specific needs and wants of the customer, then he or she may be willing to pay you a price that will include a profit for you - and to make a profit is one of the reasons you have become a home-based business owner. Although there are many activities connected with marketing, most of them can be classified in these categories: buy, finance, transport, standardize, store, insure, advertise, and sell.

Target Market Analysis

Before you can create a successful marketing campaign, it's necessary to determine your target market (toward whom to direct your energies). The whole concept of target marketing can seem very scary at first. On the surface, targeting appears to be limiting the scope of the pool of potential customers. Many people fear that by defining a market, they will lose business. They are concerned that they will choose the wrong market. The other major concerns that the other practitioners will take just anybody and therefore some of their business.

You must keep in mind that the purpose of defining your target market is to make your life easier and increase the productivity of your promotional endeavors. Many opportunities exist in this world and it's impossible to pursue them all or be everything to everyone. You need to know where to focus you energy and money when it comes to promotion and advertising.

The two most common means of market analysis are demographics and psychographics, which describe a person in terms of objective data and personality attributes.

Demographics are statistics such as:
- age
- gender
- income level
- geographic location
- occupation
- education level

Psychographics are lifestyle factors including:
- special interest activities
- philosophical beliefs
- social factors
- cultural involvements

The more you know about your potential customers, the easier it is to develop an appropriate position statement and design an effective marketing campaign. The actual number of target markets you have depends mainly upon the size of your practice and the scope of your knowledge.

Your Target Market Profile

In order to clarify your target market(s) you need to delineate the demographic and psychographic factors and then identify the characteristics your customers have in common.

Describe you current customers and those who are most likely your future customers:

What is the age range and average age of your customers?

What is the percentage of males?

What is the percentage of females?

What is the average educational level of your customers?

Where do your customers live?

What are the occupations of your customers?

Where do your customers work?

What is the average annual income level of your customers?

Of what special interest groups are your customers members?

What attitudes and beliefs about health care do your customers hold?

What is the primary reason your customers use your services?

Defining Your Target Markets(s)

Write a descriptive statement for each of your target markets (refer to your "Target Market Profile"). Include a brief overview of the services you are providing to that group and a detailed analysis of the characteristics of the specific clientele.

Target Market 1:

Target Market 2:

Target Market 3:

Home-Based Business Marketing

The foundation for creating a thriving customer base.

A. Overview
    This section is about clarifying your beliefs and attitudes toward
    your profession and determining the image you wish to portray.

    1. Describe the "character" that you want for your practice.
        Depict the image you want to convey:

    2. State your philosophy in regards to your profession:

    3. Describe your philosophy regarding your practice in
        particular:

B. Customer Profile
This is a descriptive analysis of your current and potential customers - who they are, what their interests are and where you can find them. Include each of your target markets.

1. Target Market 1:

2. Target Market 2:

3. Target Market 3:

C. Competition's Marketing Assessment
The first phase in planning your promotional campaign is appraising the competition. List each of your major competitors and describe the marketing strategies they utilize. Be certain to include where and how often they advertise.

1. Major Competitor 1:

2. Major Competitor 2:

3. Major Competitor 3:

4. Major Competitor 4:

5. Major Competitor 5:

6. Major Competitor 6:

Home-Based Marketing Planning

Outline for Marketing:

I. Produce/Service Concept:
   A. Name of produce or service
   B. Descriptive characteristics of product or service
   C. Unit sales
   D. Analysis of market trends

II. Number of Customers in Market Area:
   A. Profile of customers
   B. Average customer expenditure
   C. Total market

III. Your Market Potential:
   A. Total market divided by competition
   B. Total market multiplied by percent who will buy your product

IV. Needs of Customers:
   A. Identification
   B. Pleasure
   C. Social approval
   D. Personal interest
   E. Price

V. Direct Marketing Sources:
   A. Trade magazines
   B. Trade associates
   C. Small Business Administration (SBA)
   D. Government publications
   E. Yellow Pages
   F. Marketing directories

VI. Customer Profile:
   A. Geographical
   B. Gender
   C. Age range
   D. Income brackets
   E. Occupation
   F. Educational level

Chapter 4

Promoting the Home-Based Business

When a new home-based business is opened, the owner must be prepared to publicize the business or its chance for success will be slim. Only a few businesses - such as those with a prime location, nationally known name, or a built-in clientele - can succeed without advertising to promote market awareness and stimulate sales.

The first purpose - promoting customer awareness - applies as much to established businesses as to newcomers.

Whatever your home-based business may be, you will find it easier to retain old customers than to win new ones. When old customers move away from your area, or when their buying needs change, you need new customers to maintain your sales volume. If you expect your business to gain, you will need additional new customers. New customers are those who move into your area or who have grown into your line of products because new they can afford them or they need them. We see advertising and we hear advertising all around us, and yet that is only a part of it. Through advertising, you call the attention of customers to your products.

As a small home-based business owner, you may advertise your business through your location. People pass by and are attracted to your operation because of what you are selling. To get a better idea of what advertising is, consider some of the following functions of advertising:

1. **To inform:** Letting customers know what you have for sale through brochures, leaflets, newspapers, radio, TV, and etc.

2. **Persuade:** Persuasion is the art of leading individuals to do what you want them to do. There are sales personnel who have persuasive sales presentations, but persuasion in advertising is nonpersonal. The appeal is made through the printed or spoken words or a picture. The influence of an ad on readers occurs as purchasers choose what they want among different products, and different wants. To gain the actions you want - a sale - you must persuade a customer to examine personally what you have for sale.

3. **Reminder:** Advertising performs it's third function when it reminds those who have been persuaded to buy once that the same product will bring satisfaction. The ad will also remind a customer of the characteristics of a product purchased some time ago, and where he or she bought it. Because customers change their loyalty to a place of business, their taste for products, and often their trading area patronage, advertising is necessary to draw new customers and to hold old customers. To generate results from advertising that will be profitable to your business, you will have to produce answers to the what, where and how of advertising

What to Advertise:
The nature of your home-based business will partially answer the question "Shall I advertise goods or services?" What are the outstanding features of your business? Is it unique in any way? Doesn't it have strong points? Do you have something to offer that the competition is not able to duplicate? Answers to these questions will give you a start in deciding what to advertise.

Where to Advertise:
Of course, you will want to advertise within your marketing area, however there are a few guidelines to remember:

A. Who are your customers?
B. What is their income range?
C. Why do they buy?
D. How do they buy? Do they pay cash? Charge?
E. What is the radius of your market area?

How to Advertise:
In determining how to advertise, you will have to consider your dollar allocation for advertising and the media suitable to your particular kind of business. However, it is important to have a balance between the presentation of the product or service being advertised and the application of three basic principles.

1. Gain the attention of the audience.
2. Establish a need.
3. Tell where that need may be filled.

See Figure A for an outline of the different advertising media and Figure B for budget on media goals.

Advertising Media

Medium	Market Coverage	Type of Audience
Daily Newspaper	Single community or entire metro area; zoned editions sometimes available	General
Weekly Newspaper	Single community	Residents
Telephone Directory	Geographical area or occupational field served by the directory	Active shoppers for goods or services
Direct mail audience	Controlled by the advertiser	Controlled
Radio audience	Definable market area	Selected
Television audience	Definable market area	Various
Outdoor	Entire metro area	General auto drivers
Magazine	Entire metro area or magazine region	Selected audience

Figure B

Promotion and Advertising Plan - Home-Based Businesses

In designing your promotional plan, it's wise to use a variety of media. You must have specific goals, time lines and budgets for each marketing application.

Media	Goal	Timeline	Budget

Chapter 5

Financial Planning for Home-Based Businesses

Financial planning is the process of analyzing and monitoring the financial performance of your business so you can assess your current position and anticipate future problem areas. The daily, monthly, seasonal, and yearly operation of your business requires attention to the figures that tell you about the firm's financial health.

Maintaining good financial records is a necessary part of doing business.

The increasing number of government regulations alone makes it virtually impossible to avoid keeping detailed records. Just as important is to keep them for yourself. The success of your business depends on them. An efficient system of record keeping can help you to:

- make management decisions
- compete in the marketplace
- monitor performance
- keep track of expenses
- eliminate unprofitable merchandise
- protect your assets
- prepare you financial statements

Financial skills should include understanding of the balance sheet, the profit-and-loss statement, cash flow projection, break-even analysis, and source and application of funds. In many businesses, the husband and wife run the business; it is especially important that both of them understand financial management. Most small business owners are not accountants, but they must understand the tool of financial management if they are going to be able to measure the return on their investment. Although good records are essential to good financial planning, they alone are not enough because their full use requires interpretation and analysis. The owner/manager's financial decisions concerning return on invested funds, approaches to banks, securing greater supplier credit, raising additional equity capital and so forth, can be more successful if he takes the time to develop understanding and use of the balance sheet and profit-and-loss statement.

Balance Sheet:
The balance sheet, Figure I, shows the financial condition of a business at the end of business on a specific day. It is called a balance sheet because the total assets balance with, or are equal to, total liabilities plus owner's capital balance. Current assets are those that the owner does not anticipate holding for long. This category includes cash, finished goods in inventory, and accounts receivable. Fixed assets are long-term assets, including plant and equipment. A third possible category is the intangible asset of goodwill. Liabilities are debts owed by the business, including both accounts payable, which are usually short-term, and notes payable, which are usually long-term debts such as mortgage payments. The difference between the value of the assets and the value of the liabilities is the capital. This category includes funds invested by the owner plus accumulated profits, less withdrawals.

The Income Statement:
This statement, Figure II, is also known as a profit-and-loss (P&L) statement. It shows how a business has performed over a certain period of time. An income statement specifies sales, cost of sales, gross profit, expenses and net income or loss from operations.

Figure I

Financial Forecast

Opening Balance Sheet - Date

Assets

Current Assets

Cash and bank accounts			$
Accounts receivable			$
Inventory			$
Other current assets			$
TOTAL CURRENT ASSETS	(A)		$

Fixed Assets

Property owned			$
Furniture and equipment			$
Business automobile			$
Leasehold improvements			$
Other fixed assets			$
TOTAL FIXED ASSETS	(B)		$
TOTAL ASSETS	(A+B = X)		$

LIABILITIES

Current Liabilities (due within the next 12 months)

Bank loans			$
Other loans			$
Accounts payable			$
Other current liabilities			$
TOTAL CURRENT LIABILITIES	(C)		$

Long-term Liabilities

Mortgages			$
Long-term loans			$
Other long-term liabilities			$
TOTAL LONG-TERM LIABILITIES	(D)		$
TOTAL LIABILITIES	(C+D = Y)		$
NET WORTH	(X-Y = Z)		$
TOTAL NET WORTH AND LIABILITIES	(Y+Z)		$

Figure II

Business Income and Expense Forecast for the Next 12 Months

One year estimate ending _____, 19___

Projected Number of Clients

For your services

For your products

TOTAL NUMBER OF CLIENTS

Projected Income

Sessions   _____

Product sales   _____

Other   _____

TOTAL INCOME   _____

Projected Expenses

Start up costs $ _____

Monthly expenses (x 12) $ _____

Annual expenses $ _____

TOTAL EXPENSES $ _____

TOTAL OPERATING PROFIT (OR LOSS) $ _____

CAPITAL REQUIRED FOR THE NEXT 12 MONTHS $ _____

Home-Based Business

Start-Up Costs Worksheet	
Item	**Estimated Expense**
Open checking account	$
Telephone installation	$
Equipment	$
First & last month's rent, security deposit, etc.	$
Supplies	$
Business cards, stationery, etc.	$
Advertising and promotion package	$
Decorating and remodeling	$
Furniture and fixtures	$
Legal and professional fees	$
Insurance	$
Utility deposits	$
Beginning inventory	$
Installation of fixtures and equipment	$
Licenses and permits	$
Other	$
TOTAL	$

Fixed Annual Expense Worksheet	
Item	**Estimated Expense**
Property insurance	$
Business auto insurance	$
Licenses and permits	$
Liability insurance	$
Disability insurance	$
Professional society membership	$
Fees (legal, accounting, etc.)	$
Taxes	$
Other	$
TOTAL	$

Monthly Business Expense Worksheet		
Expense	Estimated Monthly Cost	X 12
Rent	$	$
Utilities	$	$
Telephone	$	$
Bank fees	$	$
Supplies	$	$
Stationery and business cards	$	$
Networking club dues	$	$
Education (seminars, books, professional journals, ect.)	$	$
Business car (payments, gas, repairs, etc.)	$	$
Advertising and promotion	$	$
Postage	$	$
Entertainment	$	$
Repair, cleaning and maintenance	$	$
Travel	$	$
Business loan payments	$	$
Salary/Draw	$	$
Staff salaries	$	$
Miscellaneous	$	$
Taxes	$	$
Professional fees	$	$
Decorations	$	$
Furniture and fixtures	$	$
Equipment	$	$
Inventory	$	$
Other	$	$
TOTAL MONTHLY	$	
TOTAL YEARLY		$

Cash Flow Forecast						
	January Estimate	January Actual	February Estimate	February Actual	March Estimate	March Actual
Beginning cash						
Plus monthly income from: Fees						
Sales						
Loans						
Other						
TOTAL CASH AND INCOME						
Expenses:						
Rent						
Utilities						
Telephone						
Bank fees						
Supplies						
Stationery and business cards						
Insurance						
Dues						
Education						
Auto						
Advertising and promotion						
Postage						
Entertainment						
Repair and maintenance						
Travel						
Business loan payments						
Licenses and permits						
Salary/Draw						
Staff salaries						
Taxes						
Professional fees						

Decorations						
Furniture and fixtures						
Equipment						
Inventory						
Other Expenses						
TOTAL EXPENSES						
ENDING CASH (+/-)						

Chapter 6

Home-Based Business Planning

Introduction

Homework has taken on new meaning for more than 30 million Americans. The drive for economic self-sufficiency has motivated large numbers of persons to market their skills and talents for profit from home. Our increasingly service oriented economy offers a widening spectrum of opportunities for customized and personalized small business growth.

Though untrained entrepreneurs have traditionally had a high rate of failure, small businesses can be profitable. Success in small home-based business is not an accident. It requires both skills in a service or product area and acquisition of management and attitudinal competencies.

The purpose of this publication is to help you take stock of your interests, aptitudes and skills. Many people have good business ideas but not everyone has what it takes to succeed. If you are convinced that a profitable home business is attainable, this publication will provide step-by-step guidance in development of the basic written business plan.

Information Gathering

A helpful tool for use in determining if you are ready to take the risks of a home-based business operation is the SMA publication entitled Going Into Business (MP-12).

33

It will help you focus on the basic steps in information gathering and business planning.

While the reasons for the rapid growth of home-based business operations may vary from the need to supplement family income with a few hundred dollars all the way to a sophisticated technical consulting service billing hundreds of thousands of dollars, there are many common characteristics and challenges to be considered in launching most home-based businesses, regardless of size. Some tasks are universal to all small business startups, while others are unique to a home base.

Careful planning is required to research legal and tax issues, proper space utilization and to establish time management discipline. Inadequate or careless attention to development of a detailed business plan can be costly for you and your family in terms of lost time, wasted talent and disappearing dollars.

The Entrepreneurial Personality

A variety of experts have documented research that indicates that successful small business entrepreneurs have some common characteristics. How do you measure up? On this checklist, write a "Y" if you believe the statement describes you; a "N" if it doesn't; and a "U" if you can't decide:

_____ I have a strong desire to be my own boss.

_____ Win lose or draw, I want to be master of my own financial destiny.

_____ I have significant specialized business ability based on both my education and my experience.

_____ I have an ability to conceptualize the whole of a business; not just its individual parts, but how they relate to each other.

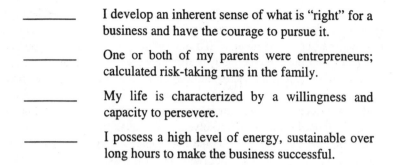

	I develop an inherent sense of what is "right" for a business and have the courage to pursue it.
	One or both of my parents were entrepreneurs; calculated risk-taking runs in the family.
	My life is characterized by a willingness and capacity to persevere.
	I possess a high level of energy, sustainable over long hours to make the business successful.

While not every successful home-based business owner starts with a "Y" answer to all of these questions, three or four "N's" and "U's" should be sufficient reason for you to stop and give second thought to going it alone. Many proprietors who sense entrepreneurial deficiencies seek extra training and support their limitations with help from a skilled team of business advisors such as accountants, bankers and attorneys.

Selecting a Business

Perhaps you have already decided what your home-based business will be. You know how you will serve your market and with what. If not, but you are determined to establish a home-based source of income, then you need to decide exactly what business you will enter. A logical first step for the undecided is to list potential areas of personal background, special training, educations and job experience, and special interests that could be developed into a business. Review the following list of activities which have proven marketable for others. On a scale of "0" (no interest or strength) to "10" (maximum interest or strength) indicate the potential for you and a total score for each activity.

Time Management

For both the novice and the experience business person planning a small home-based enterprise, an early concern requiring self-evaluation is time management.

It is very difficult for some people to make and keep work schedules even in a disciplined office setting. At home, as your own boss, the problem can be much greater. To determine how much time you can devote to your business, being by drafting a weekly task timetable listing all current and potential responsibilities and the blocks of time required for each. When and how can business responsibilities be added without undue physical or mental stress on you and your family? Potential conflicts must be faced and resolved at the outset and as they occur, otherwise your business can become a nightmare. During the first year of operation, continue to chart, post and checkoff tasks on a daily, weekly and monthly basis.

Distractions and excuses for procrastination abound. It is important to keep both a planning and operating log. These tools will help avoid oversights and provide vital information when memory fails.

To improve the quality of home work time, consider installation of a separate telephone line for the business and attach an answering machine to take messages when you do not wish to be distracted or are away from home. A business line has the added advantage of allowing you to have a business listing in the phone book and if you wish to buy it, an ad in the classified directory.

Is a Home-Based Business Site Workable?

- Where in the home will the business be located?
- What adjustments to living arrangements will re required?
- What will be the cost of changes?
- How will your family react?
- What will the neighbors think?

It will be important to set aside a specific work area. For example, more than one fledgling business ledger has gone up in smoke, been chewed by the family dog, or thrown out with the trash when business records were not kept separate from family papers. Ready access to business records during work hours is essential, but they must be protected.

Check the reasons below for and against working at home that apply to you. List any additional drawbacks or obstacles to operating this business at home.

Pros	Cons
Lower startup costs	Isolation
Lower fixed costs	Space limitations
Tax benefits	Zoning
Lifestyle flexibility	Security concerns
No commuting	Household interference

Note that changes in personal habits will be required.

Examples
- Self discipline to keep TV off while working
- Limiting personal telephone calls in length and number
- Diligence in meeting work deadlines when no one is checking

Ask family members to comment on pros and cons. Their concerns may require reconsideration of some specifics.

Is a Home-Based Business Site Allowable?

Now you will want to investigate potential legal and community problems associated with operating the business from home. You should gather, read and digest specialized information concerning federal, state, county and municipal laws and regulations concerning home-based business operations.

Check first! Get the facts in writing. Keep a topical file for future reference. Some facts and forms will be needed for your business plan. There may be limitations enforced that can make your planned business impossible or require expensive modifications to your property.

Items to be investigated, recorded and studied are:

TO DO	DONE	
_____	_____	county or city zoning code restrictions
_____	_____	necessary permits and licenses for operation
_____	_____	state and local laws and codes regarding zoning
_____	_____	deed or lease restrictions such as covenants and restrictive conditions of purchase
_____	_____	parking and customer access; deliveries
_____	_____	sanitation, traffic and noise codes
_____	_____	signs and advertising
_____	_____	state and federal code requirements for space, ventilation, heat and light
_____	_____	limitations on the number and type of workers. If not, check with the local Chamber of Commerce office
_____	_____	reservations that neighbors may have about a business next to or near them

Here are some ways to collect your information. Call or visit the zoning office at county headquarters or city hall. In some localities the city or county Office of Economic Development has print materials available to pinpoint key "code" items affecting home-based business.

Even in rural areas, the era of unlimited free enterprise is over. Although the decision makers may be in the state capital or in a distant regional office of a federal agency, check before investing in inventory, equipment or marketing programs. If in doubt, call the state office of Industrial Development or the nearest SBA district office. In some states the county agent or home demonstration agent will have helpful information concerning rural or farm business development.

38

To cover the income tax rules regarding a home-based business, be sure to secure the IRS Publication #587, BUSINESS USE OF YOUR HOME.

Is the Home-Based Business Site Insurable?

In addition to community investigations, contact your insurance company or agent. It is almost certain that significant changes will be required in your coverage and limits when you start a home-based business. When you have written a good description of your business, call you agent for help in insuring you properly against new hazards resulting from your business operations such as:

- fire, theft and casualty damage to inventories and equipment
- business interruption coverage
- fidelity bonds for employees
- liability for customers, vendors and others visiting the business
- workmen's compensation
- group health and life insurance
- product liability coverage if you make or sell a product; workmanship liability for services
- business use of vehicle coverage

Overall Home Site Evaluation

After you have gathered as much information as seems practical you may wish to evaluate a home-based site vs. one or more other nearby locations. Here's a handy checklist. Using the "0" to "10" scale, grade these vial factors:

Factors to Consider

Factor	Grades for Each	
	Home	**Other**
1. Customer convenience	_____	_____
2. Availability of merchandise or raw materials	_____	_____
3. Nearby competition	_____	_____
4. Transportation availability and rates	_____	_____
5. Quality and quantity of employees available	_____	_____
6. Availability of parking facilities	_____	_____
7. Adequacy of utilities (sewer, water, power, gas)	_____	_____
8. Traffic flow	_____	_____
9. Tax burden	_____	_____
10. Quality of police and fire services	_____	_____
11. Environmental factors	_____	_____
12. Physical suitability for future expansion	_____	_____
13. Provision for future expansion	_____	_____
14. Vendor delivery access	_____	_____
15. Personal convenience	_____	_____

16. Cost of operation   _____   _____

17. Other factors including how big
     you get without moving   _____   _____

                    TOTALS   _____   _____

Writing the Business Plan

Now that your research and plan development is nearing completion, it is time to move into action. If you are still in favor of going ahead, it is time to take several specific steps. The key one is to organize your dream scheme into a business plan.

What is it?

- As a business plan is written by the home-based business owner with outside help as needed
- It is accurate and concise as a result of careful study
- It explains how the business will function in the marketplace
- It clearly depicts its operational characteristics
- It details how it will be financed
- It outlines how it will be managed
- It is the management and financial "blueprint" for startup and profitable operation
- It serves as a prospectus for potential investors and lenders

41

Why create it?

- The process of putting the business plan together, including the thought that you put in before writing it, forces you to take an objective, critical, unemotional look at your entire business proposal
- The finished written plan is an operational tool which, when properly used, will help you manage your business and work toward its success
- The completed business plan is a means for communicating your ideas to others and provides the basis for financing your business

Who should write it?

- The home based owner to the extent possible
- Seek assistance in weak areas, such as:
  - accounting
  - insurance
  - capital requirements
  - operational forecasting
  - tax and legal requirements

When should a business plan be used?

- To make crucial startup decisions
- To reassure lenders or backers
- To measure operations progress
- To test planning assumptions
- As a basis for adjusting forecasts
- To anticipate ongoing capital and cash requirements
- As the benchmark for good operations management

Proposed Outline for Home-Based Business Plan

This outline is suggested for a small proprietorship or family business. Shape it to fit *your* unique needs. For more complex manufacturing or franchise operations see the Resource section for other options.

Part I - Business Organization

Cover page:
    A.   Business name:

        Street address:

        Mailing address:

        Telephone number:

        Owner(s) name(s):

Inside pages:
    B.   Business form:
        (proprietorship, partnership, corporation)

        If incorporated (state incorporation)

        Include copies of key subsidiary documents in an appendix. Remember even partnerships require written agreements of terms and conditions to avoid later conflicts and to establish legal entities and equities. Corporations require charters, articles of incorporation and bylaws.

Part II - Business Purpose and Function

In this section, write an accurate yet, concise description of the business. Describe the business you plan to start in narrative form.

What is the principal activity? Be specific. Give product or service description(s):

- retail sales?
- manufacturing?
- service?
- other?

How will it be started?

- a new startup
- the expansion of an existing business
- purchase of a going business
- a franchise operation
- actual or projected start up date

Why will it succeed? Promote your idea!

- how and why this business will be successful
- what is unique about your business
- what is its market "niche"

What is your experience in this business? If you have a current resume of your career, include it in an appendix and reference it here. Otherwise write a narrative here and include a resume in the finished product. If you lack specific experience, detail how you plan to gain it, such as training, apprenticeship or working with partners who have experience.

The Marketing Plan

The marketing plan is the core of you business rationale. To develop a consistent sales growth a home-based business person must become knowledgeable about the market. To demonstrate you understanding, this section of the home-based business plan should seek to concisely answer several basic questions:

Who is your market?
- Describe the profile of your typical customer
  Age?
  Male, female, both?
  How many in family?
  Annual family income?
  Location?
  Buying patterns?
  Reason to buy from you?
  Other?

- Geographically describe your trading area (i.e., county, state, national)
- Economically describe your trading area: (single family, average earnings, number of children)

How large is the market?
- Total units or dollars?
- Growing _____ Steadily _____ Decreasing _____
- If growing, annual growth rate?

Who is your competition?
No small business operates in a vacuum. Get to know and respect the competition. Target your marketing plans. Identify direct competitors (both in terms of geography and product lines), and those who are similar or marginally comparative. Begin by listing names, addresses and products or services. Detail briefly but concisely the following information concerning each of your competitors:
- Who are the nearest ones?
- How are their business similar or competitive to yours?
- Do you have a unique "niche?" Describe it.
- How will your service or product be better or more saleable than your competitors?

- Are their businesses growing? Stable? Declining? Why?
- What can be learned from observing their operations or talking to their present or former clients?
- Will you have competitive advantages or disadvantages by operating from home? Be honest!

What percent of the market will you penetrate?
1. estimate the market in total units or dollars

2. estimate your planned volume

3. amount your volume will add to total market

4. subtract 3 from 2

Item 4 represents the amount of your planned volume that must be taken away from the competition.

What pricing and sales terms are you planning?
The primary consideration in pricing a product or service is the value that it represents to the customer. If, on the previous checklist of features, your product is truly ahead of the field, you can command a premium price. On the other hand, if it is a "me too" product, you may have to "buy" a share of the market to get your foothold and then try to move price up later. This is always risky and difficult. One rule will always hold: ultimately, the market will set the price. If your selling price does not exceed your costs and expenses by the margin necessary to keep your business healthy, you will fail. Know your competitors pricing policies. Send a friend to comparison shop. Is there discounting? Special sales? Price leaders? Make some "blind" phone calls. Detail your pricing policy.

What is your sales plan?

Describe how you will sell, distribute or service what you sell. Be specific. Below are outlined some common practices:

Direct sales - by telephone or in person. The tremendous growth of individual sales representative who sell by party bookings, door to door, and through distribution of call back promotional campaigns suggests that careful research is required to be profitable.

Mail Order - Specialized markets for leisure time or unique products have grown as more two income families find less time to shop. Be aware of recent mail order legislation and regulation.

Franchising -
a. You may decide to either buy into someone else's franchise as a franchisee, or
b. Create your own franchise operation that sells rights to specific territories or product lines to others. Each will require further legal, financial and marketing research.

Management Plan

Who will do what?

Be sure to include four basic sets of information:

1. State a personal history of principals and related work, hobby or volunteer experience (include formal resumes in Appendix)

2. List and describe specific duties and responsibilities of each

3. List benefits and other forms of compensation for each

4. Identify other professional resources available to the business: Example: Accountant, lawyer, insurance broker, banker. Describe relationship of each to business: Example "Accountant available on part time hourly basis, as needed,

47

initial agreement calls for services not to exceed x hours per month at $xx.xx per hour."

To make this section graphically clear, start with a simple organizational chart that lists specific tasks and shows, *who* (type of person is more important than an individual name other than for principals) will do *what* indicated by arrows, work flow and lines of responsibility and/or communications. Consider the following examples:

Company President
(owner-manager)

Shop Manager	Sales Manager (owner-manager)	Office (owner-manager)
|	|	|

or like this?

Company President
(owner-manager)

Sales Manager	Shop Manager (owner-manager)	Office (owner-manager)
|	|	|

As the service business grows, its organization chart could look like this:

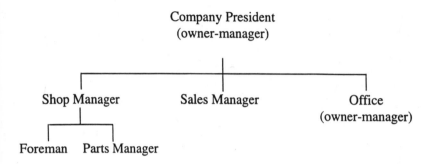

Company President
(owner-manager)

Shop Manager   Sales Manager   Office
                                              (owner-manager)

Foreman   Parts Manager

The Financial Plan

Clearly the most critical section of your business plan document is the financial plan. In formulating this part of the planning document, you will establish vital schedules that will guide the financial health of you business through the troubled waters of the first year and beyond.

Before going into the details of building the financial plan, it is important to realize that some basic knowledge of accounting is essential to the productive management of your business. If you are like most home business owners, you probably have a deep and abiding interest in the product or services that you sell or intend to sell. You like to do what you do, and it is even more fulfilling that you are making money doing it. There is nothing wrong with that. Your conviction that what you are doing or making is worthwhile is vitally important to success. Nonetheless, the income of a coach who takes the greatest pride in producing a winning team will largely depend on someone keeping score of the wins and losses.

The business owner is no different. Your product or service may improve the condition of mankind for generations to come, but, unless you have access to an unlimited bankroll, you will fail if you don't make a profit. If you don't know what's going on in your business, you are not in a very good position to assure its profitability.

Most home-based businesses will use the "cash" method of accounting with a system of record keeping that may be little more than a carefully annotated checkbook in which is recorded all receipts and all expenditures, backed up by a few forms of original entry (invoices, receipts, cash tickets). For a Sole Proprietorship, the business form assumed by this Management Aid, the very minimum of recorded information is that required to accurately complete the federal Internal Revenue Service Form 1040, Schedule C. Other business types (partnerships, joint ventures, corporations) have similar requirements but use different tax forms.

If your business is, or will be, larger than just a small supplement to family income, you will need something more sophisticated. Stationery stores can provide you with several packaged small business accounting systems complete with simple journals and ledgers and detailed instructions in understandable language.

Should you feel that your accounting knowledge is so rudimentary that you will need professional assistance to establish you accounting system, the classified section of your telephone directory can lead you to a number of small business services that offer a complete range of accounting services. You can buy as much as you need, from a simple "pegboard" system all the way to computerized accounting, tax return service and monthly profitably consultation. Rates are reasonable for the services rendered and an investigative consultation will usually be free. Look under the heading, "Business Consultants," and make some calls. Be sure to let them know the size of your business so you get tho the ones who specialize in home-based operations. Many of them are home-based entrepreneurs themselves, and know what you will be going through.

Let's start by looking at the makeup of the financial plan for the business.

The financial plan includes the following:

1. Financial Planning Assumptions - these are short statements of the conditions under which you plan to operate.
   - Market health
   - Date of startup
   - Sales buildup ($)
   - Gross profit margin
   - Equipment, furniture and fixtures required
   - Payroll and other key expenses that will impact the financial plan
2. Operations Plan - Profit and Loss Projection - this is prepared for the first year's Budget. Appendix A-11.
3. Source of Funds Schedule - this shows the source(s) of your funds to capitalize the business and how they will be distributed among your fixed assets and working capital.
4. Pro Forma balance Sheet - "Pro forma" refers to the fact that the balance sheet is before the fact, not actual. This form displays Assets, Liabilities and Equity of the business. This will indicate how much Investment will be required by the business and how much of it will be used as Working Capital in its operation.
5. Cash Flow Projection - this will forecast the flow of cash into and out of your business through the year. It helps you plan for staged purchasing, high volume months and slow periods.

Creating the Profit and Loss Projection

Appendix A-11. Create a wide sheet of analysis paper with a three inch wide column at the extreme left and thirteen narrow columns across the page. Write at the top of the first page the planned name of your business. One the second line of the heading, write "Profit and Loss Projection." One the third line, write "First Year."

Then, note the headings on Appendix A-11 and copy them onto your 12-column sheet, copy the headings from the similar area on Exhibit

A. Then follow the example set by Appendix A-11 and list all of the other components of your income, cost and expense structure. You many add or delete specific loans of expense to suit your business plan. Guard against consolidating too many types of expense under one account lest you lose control of the components. At the same time, don't try to break down expenses so discretely that accounting becomes a nuisance instead of a management tool. Once again, Exhibit A provides ample detail for most home-based businesses.

Now, in the small column just to the left of the first monthly column, you will want to note which of the items in the left-hand column are to be estimated on a monthly (M) or yearly (Y) basis. Items such as Sales, Cost of Sales and Variable Expenses will be estimated monthly based on planned volume and seasonal or other estimated fluctuations. Fixed Expenses can usually be estimated on a yearly basis and divided by twelve to arrive at even monthly values. The "M" and "Y" designations will be used later to distinguish between variable and fixed expense.

Depreciation allowances for Fixed Assets such as production equipment, office furniture and machines, vehicles, etc. will be calculated from the Source of Funds Schedule.

Appendix A-11 describes line by line how the values on the Profit and Loss Projection are developed. Use this as your guide.

Source of Funds Schedule

To create this schedule, you will need to create a list of all the Assets that you intend to use in your business, how much investment each will require and the source of funds to capitalize them. A sample of such a list is shown below:

Asset	Cost	Source of Funds
Cash	$ 2,500	Personal savings
Accounts Receivable	3,000	From profits
Inventory	2,000	Vendor credit
Pickup truck	5,000	Currently owned
Packaging machine	10,000	Installment purchase
Office desk and chair	300	Currently owned
Calculator	75	Personal cash
Electric typewriter*	500	Personal savings

*A note about office equipment: although this management aid has been written for a broad audience of home-based business operators, those who plan enterprises which produce printed products or a large volume of correspondence should consider an electronic word processor as a great time saver. Test use or rent two or more brands that appear to meet your needs and select the one with which you feel most comfortable. Don't be afraid to ask others who have had to make this decision for advice. Compatibility of your system with those of potential typesetting services or printers should be of high considerations. If you are not quite sure, consider tenting or leasing the equipment until you are. Service contracts on such complex electronic gear are usually a good insurance policy.

Before you leave your Source of Funds Schedule, indicate the number of months (years x 12) of useful life for depreciable fixed assets. (In example, the pickup truck, the packaging machine and the furniture and office equipment would be depreciable.) Generally, any individual item of equipment, furniture, fixtures, vehicles, etc., costing over $100 should be depreciated. For more information on allowances for depreciation, you can get free publications and assistance from your local Internal Revenue Service office. Divide the cost of each fixed asset item by the number or months over which it will be depreciated. You will need this data to enter as monthly depreciation on your Profit and Loss Projection. All of the data on the Source of Funds Schedule will be needed to create the Balance Sheet.

Creating the Pro Forma Balance Sheet

Appendix A-13. This is a Balance Sheet form. There are a number of variations of this form and you may find it prudent to ask your banker for the form that the bank uses for small business. It will make it easier for them to evaluate the health of your business. Use this to get started and transfer the data to your preferred form later. Accompanying Appendix A-12 which describes line by line how to develop the Balance Sheet.

Even though you may plan to stage the purchase of some assets through the year, for the purpose of this pro forma Balance Sheet, assume that all assets will be provided at the startup.

Cash Flow Projection

An important subsidiary schedule to your financial plan is a monthly Cash Flow Projection. Prudent business management practice is to keep no more cash in the business than is needed to operate it and to protect it from catastrophe. In most small businesses, the problem is rarely one of having too much cash. A Cash Flow Projections made to advise management of the amount of cash that is going to be absorbed by the operation of the business and compares it against the amount that will be available.

SBA has created an excellent form for this purpose and it is shown as Appendix B. Your projection should be prepared on 13-column analysis paper to allow for a twelve-month projection. Appendix B represents a line by line description and explanation of the components of the Cash Flow Projection which provides a step-by-step method of preparation.

Resources

Atkinson, WM. *Working at Home: Is It for You?* Dow Jones-Irwin, 1985. 162 p. (HD62.7.A85 1985)

Behr, Marion. *Women Working Home: The Homebased Business Guide and Directory.* 2nd edition. Edison, N.J., WWH Press, 1983. (HD6072.6.U5B44 1983)

Brabec, Barbara. *Homemade Money: the Definitive Guide To Success in a Home Business.* Betterway Pubines., 1984. 272p.

Davidson, Peter. *Earn Money at Home: Over 100 Ideas for Business Requiring Little or No Capital.* McGraw-Hill, 1981. 326p. (HD69.N3D37)

Delany, George. *The #1 Home Business Book.* Liberty Publ. Co., 1981. 169p. (HD8036.D44)

Edwards, Paul and Sarah. *Working From Home.* Jeremy Tarcher Inc., 1985.

Feldstein, Stuart. *Home, Inc.: How to Start and Operate a Successful Business From Your Home.* Grosset & Dunlap, 1981. 249p. (HD8036.F45 1981)

Hewes, Jeremy J. *Workheads: Living and Working in the Same Place.* Dolphin Books, 1981. 165p. (HD8037.U5H44)

Kishel, Gregory. *Dollars on Your Doorstep: The Complete Guide to Homebased Businesses.* Wiley, 1984. 1983p. (HD62.7.K575 1984)

Lieberoff, Allen J. *Climb Your Won Ladder: 101 Home Businesses That Can Make Your Wealthy.* Simon & Schuster, 1982. 242p. (HD2341.L49 1983)

Rice, Frederick H. *Starting a Home-Based Business,* University of Vermont. SBDC/DVES Burlington, VT., 1985.

Scott, Robert. *Office at Home.* Charles Scribner's Sons, 1985. 373p. (HF5547.5.S38 1985)

Tepper, Terri. *The New Entrepreneurs: Women Working From Home.* Universe Books, 1980. 238p. (HF5500.3.U54T46)

Waymon, Lynn. *Starting and Managing a Business from Your Home.* U.S. Small Business Administration, Starting and Managing Series, Vol.2, Washington, D.C., 1986.

U.S. Small Business Administration
Office of Business Development

Business Development Publication
MP15

Chapter 7

Managing The Business

Delegating work, responsibility, and authority is difficult in a small business because it means letting others make decisions which involved spending the owner/manager's money. At a minimum, he should delegate enough authority to get the work done, to allow assistants to take initiative, and to keep the operation moving in his absence. Coaching those who carry responsibility and authority in self-improvement is essential and emphasis in allowing competent assistants to perform in their own style rather than insisting that things be done exactly as the owner/manager would personally do them is important. "Let others take care of the details" is the meaning of delegating work and responsibility. In theory, the same principles for getting work done through other people apply whether you have 25 employees and one top assistant or 150 to 200 employees and several keymen yet, putting the principles into practice is often difficult.

Delegation is perhaps the hardest job owner/managers have to learn. Some never do. They insist on handling many details and work themselves into early graves. Others pay lip service to the idea but actually run a one-man shop. They give their assistants many responsibilities but little or no authority. Authority is the fuel that makes the machine go when you delegate word and responsibility. If an owner/manager is to run a successful company, he must delegate authority properly . How much authority is proper depends on your situation. At a minimum, you should delegate enough authority: (1) to get the work done, (2) to allow keymen to take initiative, (3) to keep things going in your absence.

The person who fills a key management spot in the organization must either be a manager or be capable of becoming one. A manager's chief job is to plan, direct, and coordinate the work of others. He should possess the three "I's" - Initiative, Interest, and Imagination. The manager of a department must have enough self-drive to start and keep things moving. Personality traits must be considered. A keyman should be strong-willed enough to overcome opposition when necessary.

When you manage through others, it is essential that you keep control. You do it by holding a subordinate responsible for his actions and checking the results of those actions. In controlling your assistants, try to strike a balance. You should not get into a keyman's operations so closely that you are "in his hair" nor should you be so far removed that you lose control of things.

You need feedback to keep yourself informed. Reports provide a way to get the right kind of feedback at the right time. This can be daily, weekly, or monthly depending on how soon you need the information. Each department head can report his progress, or lack of it, in the unit of production that is appropriate for his activity; for example, items packed in the shipping room, sales per territory, hours of work per employee.

For the owner/manager, delegation does not end with good control. It involves coaching as well, because management ability is not acquired automatically. You have to teach it. Just as important, you have to keep your managers informed just as you would be if you were doing their jobs.

Part of your job is to see that they get the facts they need for making their decisions. You should be certain that you convey your thinking when you coach your assistants. Sometimes words can be inconsistent with thoughts. Ask questions to make sure that the listener understands your meaning. In other words, delegation can only be effective when you have good communications.

Sometimes an owner/manager finds himself involved in many operational details even though he does everything that is necessary for delegation responsibility. In spite of defining authority, delegation, keeping control, and coaching, he is still burdened with detailed work. Usually, he had failed to do one vital thing. He has refused to stand back and let the wheels turn.

If the owner/manager is to make delegation work, he must allow his subordinates freedom to do things their way. He and the company are in trouble if he tries to measure his assistants by whether they do a particular task exactly as he would do it. They should be judged by their results - not their methods. No two persons react exactly the same in every situation. Be prepared to see some action taken differently from the way in which you would do it even though your policies are well defined. Of course, if an assistant strays too far from policy, you need to bring him back in line. You cannot afford second-guessing.

You should also keep in mind that when an owner/manager second-guesses his assistants, he risks destroying their self-confidence. If the assistant does not run his deparment to your satisfaction and if his shortcomings cannot be overcome, then replace him. But when results prove his effectiveness, it is good practice to avoid picking at each move he makes.

Chapter 8

Franchise Outline

Although the success rate for franchise-owned business is significatly better than for many other start-up businesses, success is not guaranteed. One of the biggest mistakes that you can make is to be in a hurrry to get into business.

If you shortcut your evaluation of a potential business, you might neglect to consider other franchises that are more suitable for you. Don't be "pressured" into a franchise that is not right for you.

Although most franchises are managed by reputable individuals, as in all industries, some are not. Also, some franchises could be poorly managed and financially weak.

This information will assist you in investigating your options. Questions needed to adequately evaluate the business, the franchisor, the franchise package, and ourself are included.

WHAT IS FRANCHISING?

A franchise is a legal and commerical relationship between the owner of a trademark, trade name, or advertising symbol and individial or group seeking the right to use that identification in a business. The franchise governs the method for conducting business between two parties.

While forms of franchising have been in use since the Civil War, enormous growth has occurred more recently. By the end of 1991,

600,000 establishments in 50 industries will achieve gross sales of over half a trillion dollars and employ 5.6 million full and part-time workers. Industries that rely on franchised businesses to distribute their products and services through every aspect of life from automobile sales and real estate to fast foods and tax preparation.

In the simplest form, a franchisor owns the right to a name or trademark and sells that right to a franchise. This is known as "product/trade name franchising". In the more complex form, "business format franchising," a broader and ongoing relationship exists between the two parties.

Business format franchising often provides a full range of services, including site selection, training, product supply, marketing plans, and even financing. Generally, a franchise sells goods or services that meet the franchisor's quality standards.

BENEFITS OF A FRANCHISE
There are a number of aspects to the franchising method that appeal to prospective business owners. Easy access to an established product as well as a proven method of marketing reduces the many risks of opening a business. In fact S.B.A. and Department of Commerce statistics show a significantly lower failure rate for franchisee-owned businesses than for other business start-ups.

The franchisee purchases, along with a trade-mark, the experience and expertise of the franchisor's organization. However, a franchise does not ensure easy success.

If you are not prepared for the total commitment of time, energy, and financial resources that any business requires, this is the point at which you should stop.

INVESTIGATE YOUR OPTIONS
As in all major business decisions, nothing substitutes for thorough investigation, planning, and analysis of your options. The following

information will help you set up a systematic program to analyze the possibilities and pitfalls of the franchised business you are considering.

Use the questions below to guide your research and cover all the bases. Read the full text before you begin to gather the information you will need.

SOURCES OF INFORMATION
You will need at least the following sources of information as well as experienced professional advice:

A Directory of Franchisors - The Franchise Opportunities Handbook published by the U.S. Department of Commerce is available from:

The Superintendent of Documents
U.S. Government Printing Office
Washington, D.C. 20302

Others are available at your library.

THE DISCLOSURE DOCUMENT
A Federal Trade Commisssion rule requires that franchise and business opporturnity sellers provide you a detailed disclosure document at least ten days before you pay any money or legally commit yourself to a purchase. This document includes 20 important items of information, such as:
Names, addresses, and telephone numbers of other purchasers.
A fully-audited financial statement of the seller.
The background and experience of the key executives.
The cost required to start and maintain the business.
The responsibilities you and the seller will share once you buy.

CURRENT FRANCHISEES
Talk to other owners and ask them about their experiences regarding earnings claims and information in the Disclosure Document. Be certain that you talk to franchisees and not company-owned outlets.

OTHER REFERENCES

You should get more informaiton and publications from the U.S. Small Business Administration, the Federal Trade Commission, The better Business Bureau, the local Chamber of Commerce and associations, such as:

The International Franchise Assoc.
1025 Connecticut Ave. N.W.
Washington, D.C. 20036

PROFESSIONAL ADVICE

Finally, unless you have had considerable business experience and legal training, you need a lawyer, an accountant, and a business advisor to counsel you and go over the Disclosure Document and proposed contract. Remember, the money and time you spend before it's too late may save you from a major loss on a bad investment.

WHAT IS THE BUSINESS?

Is the product or service offered new or proven? Is the product one for which you have a solid background? Do you feel a strong motivation for producing the product or providing the service?

Does the product meet a local demand?

Is there a proven market?

What is the competition?

If the product requires servicing, who bears the responsibilities covered by warrantees and guarantees? The franchisee? The franchisor? If neither, are service facilities available?

What reputation does the product enjoy?

Are suppliers available?

What reputation do they enjoy?

WHO IS THE FRANCHISOR?

Visit at least one of the firm's franchisees. Observe the operation and talk to the owner. You need to determine reputation, stability, and financial strength of the franchisor.

How long has the franchisor been in the industry? How long has the firm granted franchises?

How many franchises are there? How many in your area?

Examine the attitude of the franchisor toward you. Is the firm concerned about your qualifications? Are you being rushed to sign the agreement?

Does the firm seem interested in a long-term relationship or does that interest end with the initial fee?

Are you required to purchase supplies from the franchisor? Are the prices competitive with other suppliers?

What, if any, restrictions apply to competition with other franchisees?

What are the terms covering renewal rights? Reselling the franchise?

Again, use your professional suport to examine all of these questions. Some of the contract terms may be negotiable. Find out before you sign; otherwise, it will be too late.

PERSONAL ASSESSMENT
Finally, an examination of your own skills, abilities, and experience is perhaps your most important step. Determine exactly what you want out of life and what you are willing to sacrifice to achieve your goals.

Be honest, rigorous, and specific. Ask yourself:

Am I Qualified for this Field?
    Physically?
    By experience?
    By education?
    By learning capacity?
    Financially?

Ask yourself about the effects of this decision on your family. How will htis new life style affect them? Do they understand the risks and sacrifices, and will they suport your efforts?

Beginning a franchise business is a major decision that does not ensure easy success. However, an informed commitment of time, energy, and money by you and your family can lead to an exciting and profitable venture.

Chapter 9

Business Resource Information

Books   *Anatomy of a Business Plan.* Linda Pinson and Jerry Jennett. Fullerton, Calif.: Out of Your Mind . . . and Into the Marketplace, 1988.

How to Borrow Money from a Bank. Don H. Alexander. New York: Beaufort Books, 1984.

Basic Accounting for the Small Business. Clive G. Cornish. Seattle: Self-Counsel Press, Inc., 1984.

Becoming Self-Employed: First Han Advice from Those Who Have Done It. Susan Elliott. Blue Ridge, Penn.: Liberty (a division of TAB Books), 1987.

The Business Planning Guide: Creating a Plan for Success in Your Own Business. David H. Bangs, Jr. Dover, N.H.: Upstart Publishing Company, 1988.

The Complete No Nonsense Success Library. Steve Kahn. Stamford, Conn.: Longmeadow Press.

Complete Start-Up Kit for a Business with Your Computer. Paul and Sarah Edwards. Santa Monica, Calif.: Here's How, 1989.

Consultant's Kit: Establishing and Operating Your Successful Consulting Business. Jeffrey L. Lant. Combridge, Mass.: Jeffrey L. Lant Associates, 1981.

Developing Target Markets. John H. Melchinger. Southborough, Mass.: Educational Training Systems, Inc.

Directory of Online Databases. Santa Monica, Calif.: Caudra Associates, Inc. (Published quarterly.)

Do What You Love-The Money Will Follow. Marsha Sinetar. New York: Paulist Press, 1987.

Entrepreneural Mothers. Phyllis Gillis. New York: Rawson Associates, 1984.

How to Prosper in Your Own Business-Getting Started and Staying on Course. Brian R. Smith. Brattleboro, Vt.: The Stephen Green Press, 1981.

How to Run a Small Business. J.K. Lasser, ed. Manchester, Mo.: McGraw-Hill Book Company, 1988.

How to Start a Profitable Child Care Progrma in Your Home. Patricia Gallagher. Worcester, Penn.: Child Care and You.

How to Start a Successful Word Processing Business in Your Home. Penny McBride. P.O. Box 2133, Leucadia, CA 92024.

How to Start Your Own Bed and Breakfast: A Guide to Hosting Paying Guests in Your House or Apartment. Mary Zander. Spencertown, N.Y.: Golden Hill Press, 1985.

Ideal to Marketplace: An Inventor's Guide. Thomas R. Lampe. Los Angeles: Price Stern Sloan, 1988.

The Loan Package. Emmett Ramey and Alex Wong. Sunnyvale, Calif. Successful Business Library, 1982.

Managing the One-Person Business. Mary Jean Parson. New York: Dodd, Mead, 1987.

Marketing: Researching and Reaching Your Target Market. Linda Pinson and Jerry Jennett. Fullerton, Calif.: Out of Your Mind and . . . and Into the Marketplace, 1988.

Marketing without Advertising. Michail Phillips and Salli Rasberry. Laytonville, Calif.: In Business Bookshelf, 1986.

Marketing Your Product. Douglas A. Gray and Donald Cyr. Seattle: Self-Counsel Press Inc., 1987.

Marketing Your Service. Jean Withers and Carol Vipperman. Seattle: Self-Counsel Press Inc., 1987.

Periodicals
Business Week
1221Avenue of the Americas
New York, NY 10020
or
P.O. Box 430
Highstown, NJ 08520

Entrepreneur
2311 Pontius Avenue
Los Angeles, CA 90064

Fortune
1271 Avenue of the Americas
New York, NY 10020

The Futurist
The World Future Society
4916 St. Elmo Avenue
Bethesda, MD 20814

Harvard Business Review
P.O. Box 3000
Woburn, MA 01888

In Business
Box 351
Emmaus, PA 18049

INC.
36 Commerical Wharf Road
Boston, MA 02166

Info World
375 Cochituate Road
Fromingham, MA 01701

Modern Office Procedures
1111 Chester Avenue
Cleavland, OH 44114

Mother Earth News
P.O. Box 70
Hendersonville, NC 28739

Nation's Business
4940 Nicholson Court
Kensington, MD 20895

Newsweek
444 Madison Avenue
New York, NY 10022

The Office
1200 Summer Street
Stamford, CT 06904

Savvy
P.O. Box 2495
Boulder, CO 80322

Success
P.O. Box 33000
Bergenfield, NH 07621

Technology Review
MIT
Room 10-140
Cambridge, MA 02139

U.S. News and World Report
2300 N Street, N.W.
Washington, DC 20037

Venture
P.O. Box 3206
Harlan, IA 51537

Working Woman
342 Madison Avenue
New York, NY 10017
or
P.O. Box 10130
Des Moines, IA 50349

Mothering
P.O. Box 1690
Santa Fe, NM 87504

Direct Response Specialist
P.O. Box 1075
Tarpon Springs, FL 34286
(813) 937-3480
Monthly

Family Business Review
Family Firm Institute
P.O. Box 476
Johnstown, NY 12095
(518) 762-2853
Bimonthly

Freelance Journal
    7507 Sunset Boulevard
    Suite 213
    Los Angeles, CA 90046
    (213) 874-8281
    Bimonthly

Home Business Advisor
    NextStep Publications
    P.O. Box 41108
    Fayettevile, NC 28309
    (919) 867-2128
    8 times per year

Home Business Advocate
    Wendy Priesnitz and Associates
    195 Markville Road
    Unionville, Ontario
    Canada L3R4V8

Home Business Line
    397 Post Road
    Darien CT 06820
    (203) 655-4380
    Monthly

Home Business Monthly
    38 Briarcliffe Road
    Rochester, NY 14617
    (716) 338-1144
    Bimonthly

Home Enterprise Review
    Sharon Robinson
    P.O. Box 94028
    Washington, MI 48084
    (313) 254-3174
    Quarterly

The Front Room News
    P.O. Box 1541
    Clifton, NJ 07015-1541
    Bimonthly

Home-Work
    P.O. Box 9825
    College Station, TX 77840
    (409) 693-4753
    Monthly

Homeworking Mothers
    P.O. Box 423
    East Meadow, NY 11554
    (516) 997-7394
    Quarterly

Independent Publishers Trade Report
    Greenfield Press
    P.O. Box 176
    Southport, CT 06490
    (203) 268-4878
    Monthly

Keyboarders Connection
    P.O. Box 338
    Glen Carbon, IL 62034
    Bimonthly

Long Island Freelance Network
(a division of the National
Freelance Network)
415 Rutgers Road
West Babylon, NY 11704
(516) 422-9010
Bimonthly

Minding Your Own Business
John H. Melchinger Company
15 Cypress Street
Suite 207
Newton Centre, MA 02159-2231
(617) 969-0823
Bimonthly

Newsletters

Challenges
P.O. Box 22432
Kansas City, MO 64113-2432
(816) 363-6544
7 times per year

Direct Response Specialist
P.O. Box 1075
Tarpon Springs, FL 34286
(813) 937-3480
Monthly

Family Business Review
Family Firm Institute
P.O. Box 476
Johnstown, NY 12095
(518) 762-2853
Bimonthly

Freelance Journal
7507 Sunset Boulevard
Suite 213
Los Angeles, CA 90046
(213) 874-8281
Bimonthly

Home Business Advisor
NextStep Publications
P.O. Box 41108
Fayetteville, NC 28309
(919) 867-2128

Home Business Advocate
Wendy Priesnitz and Associates
195 Markville Road
Unionville, Ontario
Canada L3R4V8

Home Business Line
397 Post Road
Darien, CT 06820
(203) 655-4380
Monthly

Home Business Monthly
38 Briarcliffe Road
Rochester, NY 14617
(716) 338-1144
Bimonthly

Business Resource Organizations

American Business Association
292 Madison Avenue
New York, NY 10017
(212) 949 5900

American Business Women's Assn
9100 Ward Parkway, Box 8728
Kansas City, MO 64114
(816) 361-6621

American Entrepreneurs Association
2311 Pontius Avenue
Los Angeles, CA 90064
(213) 478-0437

American Federation of Small Business
407 S. Dearborn Street
Chicago, IL 60605
(312)427-0207

American Management Association
135 W. 50th Street
New York, NY 10020
(212) 586-8100

American Marketing Association
2505 S. Wacker Drive, Suite 200
Chicago, IL 60606
(312) 645-0536

American Self-Marketing Association
Old Chelsea Station Box 2016
New York, NY 10011
(212) 620-7444

American Small Business Association
    P.O. Box 612663
    Dallas, TX 75261
    (800) 227-1037

American Society of Independent Business
    777 Main Street, Suite 1600
    Fort Worth, TX 76102
    (917) 870-1880

Assn of Small Business Dev. Centers
    1313 Farnam, Suite 132
    Omaha, NE 68182
    (402) 595-2387

Best Employers Association
    4201 Birch Street
    Newport Beach, CA 92660
    (714) 756-6100

Chexchange Network
    P.O. Box 21697
    Columbus, OH 21697
    (614) 292-4985

Coalition of Women in National and Int'l Business
    P.O. Box 950
    Boston, MA 02119
    (617) 265-5269

Continental Assn of Resolute Employers
    101 Petaluma Boulevard N
    Petaluma, CA 94952
    (707) 778-8600

73

Council of Better Business Bureaus
1515 Wilson Boulevard
Arlington, VA 22209
(703) 276-0100

Entrepreneurs of America
2020 Pennsylvania Ave, NW, Suite 224
Washington, DE 20006
(800) 533-2665

Entrepreneurship Institute
3592 Corporate Drive, Suite 112
Columbus, OH 43231
(614) 8951153

Government Printing Office
Superintendent of Documents
Washington, DC 20402
(202) 783-3238

Health Insurance Assn of America
1025 Connecticut Ave. NW, Suite 1200
Washington, DC 20036

Insurance Information Institute
110 Williams Street
New York, NY 10038
(212) 669-9200

Int'l Assn of Business
701 Highlander Boulevard, Suite 200
Arlington, VA 76015
(703) 465-2922

Int'l Council of Small Business
  3674 Lindell Boulevard
  St. Louis, MO 63108
  (314)658-3896

Nat'l Assn of Small Business Investment Companies
  1199 N. Fairfax St, Suite 200
  Alexandria, VA 22314
  (703) 683-1601

Nat'l Assn of Home Based Businesses
  10451 Mill Run Circle, Suite 40
  Owings Mills, MD 21117
  (410) 363-3698

Nat'l Business Incubation Assn
  20 E. Circle Dr., Suite 190
  Athens, OH 45701

National Alliance of Small Business
  1825 Eye Street NW, Suite 400
  Washington, DC 20077-2740

National Assn for Business Org.
  P.O. Box 30149
  Baltimore, MD 21270
  (301) 446-8070

National Assn for Female Executives
  127 W. 24th Street
  New York, NY 10011
  (212) 645-0770

National Assn for the Cottage Industry
P.O. Box 14460
Chicago, IL 60614
(312) 472-9116

National Assn for the Self-Employed
P.O. Box 612067
Dallas, TX 75261
(800) 232-6273

National Assn of Private Enterprise
P.O. Box 470398
Ft. Worth, TX 76147
(817) 870-1971

National Assn of Women Business Owners
1010 Wayne Ave, Suite 900
Silver Spring, MD 20910
(301) 608-2590

National Business Association
15770 N. Dallas Parkway, Suite 260
Dallas, TX 75248
(214) 991-5381

National Federation of Independent Business (NFIB)
150 W. 20th Avenue
San Mateo, CA 94403
(415) 341-7441

National Insurance Consumer's Org.
121 N. Payne Street
Alexandria, VA 22314
(703) 549-8050

National Small Business Association
   1640 K Street NW
   Washington, DC 20006
   (202) 293-8830

National Small Business Benefits Assn
   9933 Lawler Avenue #210
   Skokie, IL 70077
   (312) 679-1499

Network of Small Business
   5420 Mayfield Road, Suite 205
   Lyndhurst, OH 44124
   (216) 442-5000

Public Information Department New York Federal Reserve Bank
   33 Liberty St.
   New York, NY 10045

Service Corps of Retired Executives
   1825 Connecticut Ave, NW, Suite 503
   Washington, DC 20009
   (800) 368-5855

Small Business Assistance Center
   P.O. Box 1441
   Worchester, MA 01601
   (508) 756-3513

Small Business Foundation of America Research Inst. for
Emerging Enterprises
   1155 15th St. NW
   Washington, DC 20005
   (800) 243-7232

Small Business Legislative Council
  1156 15th St. NW Ste 510
  Washington, DC 20005
  (202) 639-8500

Small Business Network
  P.O. Box 30149
  Baltimore, MD 21270
  (301) 466-8070

Small Business Service Bureau
  554 Main Street, Box 1441
  Worcester, MA 01601-1441
  (508) 756-3513

Small Business Support Center Assn
  8811 Westheimer Road # 210
  Houston, TX 77063-3617

Support Services Alliance
  P.O. Box 130
  Schoharie, NY 12157
  (518) 295-7966

U.S. Chamber of Commerce
  1615 H Street NW
  Washington, DC 20062
  (800) 638-6582

U.S. Department of Commerce Business Asssistance
  Washington, DC 20230
  (202) 377-3176

U.S. Department of the Treasury Internal Revenue Service
  P.O. Box 25866
  Richmond, VA 23289
  (800) 829-3676

U.S. Small Business Administration
  409 Third St., SW
  Washington, DC 20416
  (800) 827-5722

Chapter 10

Home-Based
Small Business
Computer Information

Selecting The Right Computer System For Your Business

Two options for your own in-house computer system are the **Minicomputer** and the **Microcomputer**.

A *Minicomputer* is a general purpose computer that can be programmed to do a variety of tasks and is generally designed so input can be entered directly into the system. For example, data such as a sales order is put into the computer at the same time the order is written. A minicomputer can be operated by users who don't have special computer knowledge. The costs for minicomputer equipment begin around $25,000, and range to above $200,000. However, costs are decreasing rapidly, so inquire for the latest estimates.

The *Micro* or *Personal Computer* is a household word if not quite yet a universal household system. It is inexpensive, small, lightweight and can be set on a desk. Such computers run programs that do an astonishing variety of tasks and can be easily operated by personnel who do not have special computer knowledge. Prices for personal computers begin at $1,500. They can satisfy the needs of many small business owners. The micro or PC usually handles one task at a time. Some may have modest capabilities for multi-tasking and multi-user applications (more than one program and terminal at one time). There are super micros with multi-tasking and networking capabilities. These cost $5,000 and up and can be used by multi-departmented companies.

Choosing The Right Computer

To *"computerize"* your business you will have to choose the right programs, select the right equipment, and implement the various application. This involves training personnel, keeping up security, maintaining equipment, supplies, and day to day operations. If you follow a well laid out plan and make well informed choices, your computer system should provide the information and control intended.

Hardware: Component	Function
Central Processing Unit (CPU)	The CPU performs logic calculations, manages the flow of data within the computer, and executes the program instructions.
Main Memory	Memory is measured in the "K" you'll often hear mentioned - for example 32K (32,000 positions). It is simply a storage area readily accessible to the CPU.
Mass Storage	This storage is simply *"nonmain."* There are a number of devices available, such as disk, diskette, and magnetic tape.
Input Device(s)	These units are used to enter data into the system for processing. An input device commonly used with computers is an combination keyboard and television-like display screen called a CRT (cathode ray tube.)
Output Device(s)	These display the data. The most common output device is a printer.

In addition to printed matter, make a list of information you would like to see displayed on the computer video screen (CRT). Again, design an hand-drown version. List the circumstances under which you would like to see this information displayed.

Choosing The Right Programs (Software)

A program is a set of instructions that tells the computer to do a particular task. Programs are written in a language (such as FORTRAN, COBOL, BASIC) that is easy for people to work with. these programs are usually referred to as *software*.

The software determines what data or information is to be entered into the computer and what output or report is to be returned by the computer after it has performed as instructed by the program. The act of entering information into a computer is called inputting the data.

Generally, there are three types of software:

Compilers and Interpreters - special software that translates programs written in people language (such as FORTRAN, COBOL, BASIC) into machine language that the CPU can execute.

Operating System Software - the programs that control all the separate component parts of the computer, such as the printer and disk drives, and how they work together. Systems software generally comes with the computer and must be present before the application software can work.

Application Software - software composed of programs that make the computer perform particular functions such as payroll check writing, accounts receivable posing or inventory reporting. Application software programs, particularly the more specialized ones, are normally purchased separately from the computer hardware.

Because the application software provides the features that will assist you and your business, it should always be evaluated and decided upon before you look at computer equipment. Before beginning your search for application software that is right for you, identify *what the software will have to accomplish.* Your time will be well spent if you research and write down your requirements.

Evaluate Your Choices

If after compiling all of your information, you find your needs are fairly complex, you may wish to engage the services of a small business consultant to assist you in evaluating your software requirements. Or you can submit the list to software retailers, custom software vendors, or mail order software houses. They, in turn should provide you with software that meets as many of your requirements as possible.

At this point you will have to review the software and verify for yourself the extent to which it actually meets your needs. Ask yourself these questions: Does it cover all of my *"musts"*? How many of my other requirements does it fulfill? Does it provide me with additional features I had not thought of earlier by now believe to be important?

After you have found one or more software packages that fit your needs, there are other general features you should check out before you make your final decision to buy a computer.

- Does it come with effective documentation? Is the operating manual written for the novice? Is the information organized so you can use it effectively after you become an experienced user?

- How easy if the software to user (user-friendly)? Does the information that is displayed on the computer screen make sense? Is there a *"help"* facility?

- How easy is it to change? Can you change data that has already been processed? Can you yourself change the "program" instructions such as payroll withholding rates, or will you have to pay the vendor to change these for you? If yes, what will it cost?

- Will you be required to change any of your business practices? If so, are these changes that you should make anyway? Will it provide the accounting and management information you need?

- How well is the software documented? You should be able to understand the general flow of information: which program does what and when.

- Does it have security features such as passwords, or user identification codes? Can it prevent unauthorized access to private information?

- Is it easy to increase the size of files?

- Will the software vendor support the software? Does the vendor have a good track record? Will the vendor make changes, and if so, how much will the changes cost?

- How long has the vendor been in business? What are the vendor's prospects for staying in business?

Selecting The Right Equipment (Hardware)

Choosing the software is by far the most difficult job in deciding upon the computer system that is right for you. Because most software is written for one, or several specific computers, you will probably have narrowed your equipment choices down considerably by the time you have selected your software.

You should review the choices and ask the same questions about potential computer hardware vendors that you asked when evaluating software vendors. Don't forget to check the cost of shipping, installation and equipment maintenance.

The computer and associated equipment known as hardware consists of a number of components, each doing a different job. The include:

Processor - The *"thinking"* part of the computer is known as the processor, or Central Processing Unit (CPU) and is designed to execute software instructions, perform calculations, control the flow of data to and from the memory, and control other hardware components.

Computer Memory - Computer memory usually is measured in bytes (which is a grouping of binary digits or bits). Roughly speaking, each byte of memory holds one character of data, either a letter or a number. A 2K (2,000 bytes) memory in practical terms holds about one double spaced typed page. There are two kinds of memory, *ROM (Read-Only Memory)* and *RAM (Random Access Memory)*.

ROM is a program stored in the computer memory and cannot be changed by the user or an externally entered program.

RAM - Random Access Memory is located in the central Processing Unit (CPU) and is normally measured in "K's" or 1000,s (64K = approximately 64,000 characters or about 32 pages of information). RAM is used to store all the information necessary for the CPU to do its job: the program running the portion of data that is currently being processed and some portion of the system software. **Information stored in RAM lasts only as long as the power is on.** Once the power is turned off, all RAM information is erased.

DOS is software that controls the interactions among the CPU, disk drive, keyboard, video monitor and printer. These two, the DOS and applications program, may need about 55K.

Evaluating the Computer System

The most important step in judging a minicomputer system is to visit a few companies using the minicomputer system you think you'll get. Visit these companies without the sales representative for the system, and try to find companies with configurations and applications as close to yours as possible.

Use the following criteria, listed in order of importance, to evaluate a minicomputer system.

1. Software Developer's Past Performance Record

   Software developer should have prior experience with similar applications for the same equipment configuration.

2. Commitment of Hardware Vendor

   Where will your commission sales rep be after the contract is signed? How many systems engineers does the vendor have in your local area?

3. Hardware Capacity

   Does the hardware have adequate processing capability to meet your requirements within the acceptable time frames?

4. Quality of Systems Software

   The quality of the system software (operating systems and utilities) dramatically affects how difficult the system is to program and use.

5.	Systems Documentation	What kind of systems documentation does the vendor provide and how is it updated? Can it be understood at some basic level by the user? Is it designed so other experts can understand how things were done and change them when necessary?
6.	Service and Maintenance Support	When your system breaks down, how long will it take to get it fixed? Who will do it? Will it be subcontracted? Are there any provisions for backup during down time?
7.	Expandability and Compatibilities	What are the technical limits of your system and how close to those limits is your current configurations? Is there software compatibility among the vendor's product lines?
8.	Security	What security features will your system have to prevent unauthorized use of the system or unauthorized program modifications?
9.	Financial Stability of Vendors	Satisfy yourself about the financial stability of your vendor.
10.	Environmental Requirements	Mini and Microcomputers do not require special environments such as raised floor, special wiring or special air conditioning. Some may, however, and it pays to find out in advance.
11.	Price	With computers you generally get what

you pay for. Low price alone should not be a prime evaluation criterion.

Implementation

As we suggested before, successful computer applications for your business depend heavily on the implementation process. Problems are inevitable but proper planning can help avoid some of them and mitigate the effects of others.

After the software and hardware choices have been made, you will need to prepare your business for the new system. One vital point to keep in mind: successful implementation of a computer system in a small business requires intense involvement of the owner-manager from the initial decision to acquire a computer through system specification, selection and implementation. Also the success of the new computer system will be directly related to the cooperation of a number of your employees; therefore it is important to involve them as early as possible with the steps to be taken. Explain to each affected employee how his or her position will change. To those unaffected, explain why their jobs will remain unchanged.

Set target dates for key phases of implementation (especially the last date for format changes).

Prepare the installation site. Check the hardware manual to be sure the location where you will keep your new computer meets the system's requirements for temperature, humidity and electrical power.

Prepare a prioritized list of applications to be converted from manual to computer systems. It is very important to plan on converting them one at a time, not all at once.

Prepare a list of all your business procedures that will be changed so the computer system will fit into the regular work flow. Develop new manual procedures to interface with the computer system.

- *Data Safety* - Date, confidential or otherwise, can be destroyed by unexpected disasters (fire, water, power fluctuations, magnetic fields, etc.) or employee tampering and could result in high costs to recreate. The best and cheapest insurance against the high cost of lost data is to keep back-up copies of all data and programs. The information on each diskette should be backed up regularly and as often as necessary to minimize the cost of recreating lost information. Copies should be kept in a safe place away from the business.

A Quick Review: What To Consider When Buying

Needs
Business operations to be done

Costs
Comparative cost vs. comparative capabilities

Memory
Capacity of RAM
Capacity of ROM

Disk Drives
Bit capacity
Multiple drives

Keyboard
Typewriter style

Software
Disk and cartridge

Number of programs written for or compatible with the PC you are interested in

Display
Color or black and white
Resolution quality
Graphics capability

Expandability
Connections for add-ons and attachments
Compatibility with other manufacturers' equipment

Supplies
Custom forms
Printer paper
Furniture
Accessories
  Disks
  Dust Covers

Repair and Training
Compare service contracts
Training provided, how much

U.S. Small Business Administration
Office of Business Development

Business Development Publication MP 14

Appendix A

A Concise Guide To Starting Your Own Business

Guide Overview

A concise overview of the complete guide to starting and operating a successful business.

The following topics are presented:

- Business Plan for Small Businesses.
- Getting Started
- Deciding Where To Start The Business
- Business Patronage Statistics
- Site Location
- Site Selection Criteria — Some General Questions.
- Choosing The Proper Method of Organization
- What Is A Corporation?
- Estimating Startup Costs
- Preparing An Income Statement
- Preparing A Balance Sheet
- Marketing The Business
- Marketing Planning — An Outline for Marketing.
- Advertising Media
- Management and Getting The Work Done
- Sample Organization Chart
- Summary of The Business Plan
- Guide Summary
- Reference Materials

Business Plan For Small Businesses

I. Type of Business

II. Location

III. Target Market

IV. Planning Process

V. Organizational Structure

VI. Staffing Procedures

VII. Control

VIII. Market Strategy

IX. Financial Planning

X. Budgeted Balance Sheet

XI. Budgeted Income Statement

XII. Budgeted Cash Flow Statement

XIII. Break-even Chart

Getting Started

Following is a list of what you need to accomplish to insure that your business endeavor will head in the right direction:

1. Define your educational background and work experience.

2. Survey all basic types of businesses.

3. Define what type of business matches your experience and educational background.

4. Choose only the business that you would like to own and operate.

5. Define what products or services your business will be marketing

6. Define who will be using your products/services.

7. Define why they will be purchasing your products/services.

8. List all competitors in your marketing area.

Deciding Where To Start The Business

Will your business fulfill a need in the area you plan to bring your business to? This section provides you with some important information you need to examine before taking your ideas any further:

1. Decide where you want to live.

2. Choose several areas that would match your priorities.

3. Use the list that follows as a guide to see if your location will match the estimated population needed to support your business. The numbers which follow the type of business indicate the typical number of inhabitants per year.

Business Patronage Statistics

Food Stores
Grocery Stores 1,534
Meat and Fish
(Sea Food) Markets 17,876
Candy, Nut, and
Confectionery Stores 31,409
Retail Bakeries 12,563
Dairy Products Stores 41,587

Eating and Drinking
Restaurant, Lunch Rooms 1,583
Cafeterias 19,341
Refreshment Places 3,622
Drinking Places 2,414

General Merchandise
Variety Stores 10,373
General Merchandise 9,837

Apparel/ Accessories Stores
Women's Ready-To
Wear Stores 7,102
Women's Accessory and
Specialty Stores 25,824
Men's And Boy's Clothing
and Furnishings 11,832
Family Clothing 16,890
Shoe Stores 9,350

**Furniture, Home Furnishings, and
Equipment Stores**
Furniture Stores 7,210
Floor Covering 29,543
Drapery, Curtains, and
Upholstery Stores 62,585
House. Appliances 12,485
Radios and T.V.'s 20,346
Record Shops 112,144
Musical Instruments 46,332

**Building Materials, Hardware, and
Farm Equipment Dealers**
Lumber and other Building
Materials Dealers 8,124
Paint, Glass, and Wallpaper
Stores 22,454
Hardware Stores 10,206
Farm Equipment Dealers 14,793

Automotive Dealers
Motor Vehicle Dealers,
New and Used Cars 6,000
Motor Vehicle Dealers,
Used Cares only 17,160
Tire, battery, and
Accessory Dealers 8,800

Boat Dealers 61,500

Household Trailer Dealers 44,746

Gasoline Service Stations 1,395

Miscellaneous
Antique and Secondhand
Stores 17,170
Book and Stationery Stores .. 28,580
Drugstores 4,268
Florists 13,531
Fuel Oil Dealers 25,000
Garden Supply Stores 65,000
Gift, Novelty Shops 26,000
Hobby, Toy, and Game
Shops 61,000
Jewelry Stores 13,400
Optical Goods Stores 62,800
Sporting Goods Stores 27,000

From *Starting and Managing a Small Business of Your Own, 1973;*
Small Business Administration, Washington, D.C.

Site Location

1. Define your number of inhabitants per store.
2. Locate several sites/locations that will match your inhabitants per store.
3. Define population and its growth potential.
4. Define local ordinances and zoning regulations that you will need in order to start your type of business.
5. Define your trading area and all competitors in your trading area.
6. Define parking need, for your kind of business.
7. Define special needs, etc., lighting, heating, ventilation.
8. Define rental cost of site/location.
9. Define why customers will come to your site/location.
10. Define the future of your site/location as to population growth.
11. Define your space needs and match with site/location selection.
12. Define the image of your business and make sure it matches your site/location.

Site Selection Criteria — Some General Questions

- Is the site centrally located to reach my market?
- What is the transportation availability and what are the rates?
- What provisions for future expansion can I make?
- What is the topography of the site (slope and foundation)?
- What is the housing availability for workers and managers?
- What environmental factors (schools, cultural, community atmosphere) might affect my business and my employees?
- What will the quality of this site be in 5 years, 10 years, 25 years?
- What is my estimate of this site in relation to my major competitor?
- What is the newspaper circulation? Are there concentrations of circulation?
- What other media are available for advertising? How many radio and television stations are there?
- Is the quantity and quality of available labor concentrated in a given area in the city or town? If so, is commuting a way of living in that city or town?
- Is the city centrally located to my suppliers?
- What are the labor conditions, including such things as relationships with the business community and average wages and salaries paid?
- Is the local business climate healthy, or are business failures especially high in the area?
- What about tax requirements? Is there a city business tax? Income tax? What is the property tax rate? Is there a personal property tax? Are there other special taxes?
- Is the available police and fire protection adequate?
- Is the city or town basically well planned and managed in terms of such items as electric power, sewage, and paved streets and sidewalks?

Choosing the Proper Method of Organization

Listed below are legal forms of business available to the small business entreprenuer:

Sole Proprietorship	
Advantages	**Disadvantages**
• Simple to start	• Unlimited liability
• All profits to owner	• "Jack-of-all-trades"
• Owner in direct control	• Capital requirement limited
• Easy entry and exit	• Limited life
• Taxed as individual	• Employee turn-over

Partnership	
Advantages	**Disadvantages**
• Easy to originate	• Unlimited liability
• Credit rating	• Misunderstandings
• Talent combination	• Partner withdrawal
• Legal contract	• Regulations

Corporation	
Advantages	**Disadvantages**
• Limited liability	• Double taxation
• Expansion potential	• Charter restrictions
• Transfer of ownership	• Employee motivation
• Retain employees	• Legal regulations

What Is A Corporation?

"A corporation is an artificial being, invisible, intangible, and existing only in contemplation of the law," wrote Chief Justice John Marshall. In other words, the corporation exists as a separate entity apart from its owners, the shareholders. It makes contracts; it is liable; it pays taxes. It is a "legal person".

The corporation is the most complex of the three major forms of business ownership. The corporation stands as a separate legal entity in the eyes of the law. The life of the corporation is independent of the owners' lives. Because the owners, called shareholders, are legally separate from the corporation, they can sell their interests in the business without affecting the continuation of the business. When a corporation is founded, it accepts the regulations and restrictions placed on it by the state in which it is incorporated and any other state in which it chooses to do business. Generally, the corporation must report its financial operations to the state's attorney general on an annual basis.

Estimating Startup Costs

Item	Amount
Fixtures and Equipment	$_____
Building & Land (If Needed)	_____
Store and/or Office Supplies	_____
Remodeling and Decorating	_____
Deposits on Utilities	_____
Insurance	_____
Installation of Fixtures	_____
Legal Fees	_____
Professional Fees	_____
Telephone	_____
Rental	_____
Salaries and Wages	_____
Inventory if Retailing	_____
Licenses and Permits	_____
Advertising and Promotion	_____
TOTAL Estimated Startup Cost	$_____

Preparing An Income Statement

What is an Income Statement?

The income statement shows the income received and the expenses incurred over a period of time. Income received (sales) comes essentially from the sales of the merchandise or service which your business is formed to sell. Expenses incurred are the expired costs that have been incurred during the same period of time.

Plan A Budgeted Income Statement For One Year

1. Project Total Sales
2. Estimate Total Expenditures
3. Example Listed Below for Income Statement

Percents	1	2	3	4	5	6	7	8	9	10	11	12
Sales												
Cost of Sales												
Gross Profit												
Expenditure												
Rent Expense												
Supplies												
Wages/Salaries												
Utilities												
Insurance												
Depreciation												
Interest												
Miscellaneous												
Net Profit												

Preparing A
Balance Sheet

What Is A Balance Sheet?

The balance sheet shows the assets, liabilities and owner's net worth in a business as of a given date.

- Assets are the things owned by your business, including both physical things and claims against others.
- Liabilities are the amounts owed to others, the creditors of the firm.
- Net worth or owner's equity is the owner's claim to the assets after liabilities are accounted for.

A Budgeted Balance Sheet For One Year

- List all your business property at their cost to you: these are your assets.
- List all debts, or what your business owes on all your property; these are your liabilities.
- Take your total property balance (Assets), and subtract the total amount you owe (Liabilities).
- The balance is what you own in your business called (Owner's equity).
- Add Total Liabilities (2) & Total Owner's Equity (3).
- Listed on the next page is an example of a balance sheet.

NAME OF BUSINESS
BALANCE SHEET
DATE

ASSETS
  Current Assets
    Cash
    Accounts Receivable
    Merchandise Inventories
      TOTAL CURRENT ASSETS

  Fixed Assets
    Land
    Building
    Equipment
      TOTAL FIXED ASSETS
        TOTAL ASSETS   1)._____

LIABILITIES
  Current Liabilities
    Accounts Payable
    Note Payable
    Payroll Taxes Payable
      TOTAL CURRENT LIABILITIES

  Long-term Liabilities
    Mortgage Payable
    Long Term Note
      TOTAL LONG-TERM LIABILITIES
        TOTAL LIABILITIES   2)._____

OWNER'S EQUITY
  Proprietor's Capital   3)._____

              TOTAL LIABILITIES & OWNER'S EQUITY   (2 & 3)._____

Marketing The Business

1. Define Your Market
   - Type of Customers
   - Age, Income, Occupation of your customers
   - Type of Trading Area

2. Promotion of Your Business
   - Advertising
   - Setting your Image

3. Customer Policy Plan
   - Develop a Customer Profile
   - Customer Services
   - Customer Needs

4. Pricing Your Products/Services
   - Know all your Costs
   - Know your Profit Margin
   - Know Competitor's Price
   - Know what Return you want on your Investment

5. Sales Promotion
   - Coupons
   - Contests
   - Displays
   - Demonstrations
   - Giveaways
   - Banners

6. Public Relations
   - Newspaper Article
   - Contact Trade Association
   - Radio Promotion
   - T.V. Promotion

7. Segmentation of your Market
   - Age
   - Occupation
   - Income
   - Location
   - Education
   - Hobbies

Marketing Planning

Outline for Marketing

I. Product/Service Concept:
    a. Name of product or service
    b. Descriptive characteristics of product or service
    c. Unit sales
    d. Analysis of market trends

II. Number of Customers in your Market Area:
    a. Profile of customers
    b. Average customer expenditure
    c. Total market

III. Your Market Potential:
    a. Total market divided by competition
    b. Total market multiplied by percent who will buy your product

IV. Needs of Customers:
    a. Identification
    b. Pleasure
    c. Social approval
    d. Personal interest
    e. Price

V. Direct Marketing Sources:
    a. Trade magazines
    b. Trade associations
    c. Small Business Administration (SBA)
    d. Government Publications
    e. Yellow pages
    f. Marketing directories

VI. Customer Profile:
    a. Geographical
    b. Gender
    c. Age range
    d. Income brackets
    e. Occupation
    f. Educational level

Advertising Media

Medium	Market Coverage	Type of Audience
Daily newspaper	Single community or entire metro area; zoned editions sometimes available	General
Weekly newspaper	Single community	Residents
Telephone directory	Geographical area or occupational field served by the directory	Active shoppers for goods or services
Direct mail audience	Controlled by the advertiser	Controlled
Radio audience	Definable market area	Selected
Television audience	Definable market area surrounding T.V. Stations	Various
Outdoor	Entire metro area	General auto drivers
Magazine	Entire metro area or magazine region	Selected audience

Management and Getting the Work Done

1. Define your objective for starting your business.

2. Define your goals: profit growth for first three years.

3. Develop an organization chart of your business.

4. Define your personal needs.
   - Hiring proper employees
   - Training employees
   - Motivation

5. Define all responsibility for each person in your business.

6. Define all authority.
   - Who will hire and fire?
   - Who will select and train all personnel?
   - Who will keep the important records as to inventory, purchasing, sales records, cash records, etc.?

7. Define all laws and regulations that will be requirements for operating your business.

8. Review all duties and tasks with all your employees.

9. Write a summary of all the important tasks that you want to finish in your first year in business.

Sample Organization Chart

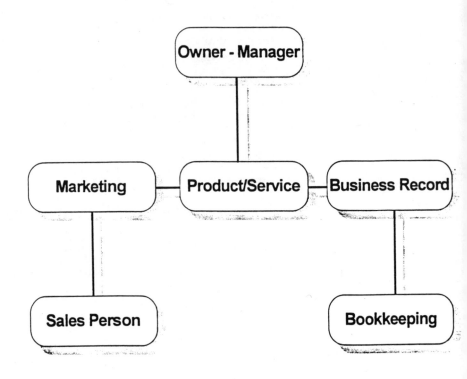

Summary of The Business Plan

Name of Business
BUSINESS PLAN
Date

1. Define your business
   - Name all principals
   - Address and phone number

2. Define your products or services

3. Define your market

4. Define your site or location

5. Advertising Plan
   - Budget
   - Media

6. Chart of Start-up cost

7. Worksheet of Income Statement
   - Revenue/Income
   - Expenses

8. Worksheet of Balance Sheet
   - Assets (Property)
   - Capital (Owner's Equity)
   - Liabilities (Debts)

9. Personnel Outline
   - Number of Employees
   - Staffing & Training

10. Management Organization
    - Organization Chart
    - Evaluation Policy
    - Job Profile

11. Special Statement
    - 3-Year Sales Schedule
    - Cash Flow
    - 3-Year Expense Schedule

Appendix B

HOUSEHOLD NEEDS

Many small business start-ups fail due to their inability to support their owners. Rarely do new businesses support their owners from the start. However, many individuals fail to recognize this fact. In addition, then, to a sound business plan, it is necessary for an owner to project the household cash needs month-by-month for the first three years of the business' operation. As a new business owner, you should be able to support yourself until your new business is able to support you in a manner to which you are accustomed.

MONTHLY HOUSEHOLD CASH NEEDS

Regular NON-BUSINESS Income
Spouse's salary   _____
Investment income   _____
Social security
Other income   _____
Retirement benefits   _____
Less taxes   _____
Net monthly income   _____

Regular Monthly Expenses

Housing
   Mortgage/Rent   _____
   Utilities   _____
   Homeowner's insurance   _____
   Property taxes   _____
   Home repairs   _____

Living Expenses
   Groceries   _____
   Telephone   _____
   Tuition   _____
   Transportation   _____
   Meals   _____
   Child care   _____
   Medical expenses   _____
   Clothing   _____
   Personal   _____

Insurance Premiums
   Life insurance   _____
   Disability insurance   _____
   Auto insurance   _____
   Medical insurance   _____

Debt Repayment
   Auto loans   _____
   Consumer debt   _____

Discretionary Expenses
   Entertainment   _____
   Vacation   _____
   Gifts   _____
   Retirement contributions   _____
   Investment savings   _____
   Charitable contributions   _____
   Dues, magazines, etc.   _____
   Professional fees   _____
   Other   _____

Total Monthly Expenses   _____

Monthly Surplus/Deficit   _____

Total Year Surplus/Deficit   _____
   (Monthly × 12)

Available Assets to Cover Deficit
   Checking accounts   _____
   Savings accounts   _____
   Money market accounts   _____
   Personal credit lines   _____
   Marketable securities   _____
   Lump-sum retirement/
     severance
   Other assets   _____

Total Assets   _____

NEEDED RESERVES
   Total Assets-Deficit   _____

PERSONAL FINANCIAL STATEMENT

This is a picture of your personal financial condition to date. It is a very important part of any loan application and/or interview, especially when a loan for a projected new business is under consideration.

PERSONAL FINANCIAL STATEMENT

_____ _____, 19____

Assets

Cash	$_____
Savings accounts	_____
Stocks, bonds, other securities	_____
Accounts/Notes receivable	_____
Life insurance cash value	_____
Rebates/Refunds	_____
Autos/Other vehicles	_____
Real estate	_____
Vested pension plan/Retirement accounts	_____
Other assets	_____
TOTAL ASSETS	$_____

Liabilities

Accounts payable	$_____
Contracts payable	_____
Notes payable	_____
Taxes	_____
Real estate loans	_____
Other liabilities	_____
TOTAL LIABILITIES	$_____

TOTAL ASSETS	$_____
LESS TOTAL LIABILITIES	$_____
NET WORTH	$_____

BALANCE SHEET

A balance sheet is a current financial statement. It is a dollars and cents description of your business (existing or projected) which lists all of its assets and liabilities.

BALANCE SHEET

_____ _____, 19____

	YEAR I	YEAR II
Current Assets		
Cash	$_____	$_____
Accounts receivable	_____	_____
Inventory	_____	_____
Fixed Assets		
Real estate	_____	_____
Fixtures and equipment	_____	_____
Vehicles	_____	_____
Other Assets		
License	_____	_____
Goodwill	_____	_____
TOTAL ASSETS	$_____	$_____
Current Liabilities		
Notes payable (due within 1 year)	$_____	$_____
Accounts payable	_____	_____
Accrued expenses	_____	_____
Taxes owed	_____	_____
Long-Term Liabilities		
Notes payable (due after 1 year)	_____	_____
Other	_____	_____
TOTAL LIABILITIES	$_____	$_____
NET WORTH (ASSETS minus LIABILITIES)	$_____	$_____

TOTAL LIABILITIES plus NET WORTH should equal ASSETS

PROFIT AND LOSS STATEMENT

A profit and loss statement is a detailed earnings statement for the previous full year (if you are already in business). Existing businesses are also required to show a profit and loss statement for the current period to the date of the balance sheet.

PROJECTED PROFIT AND LOSS STATEMENT

	Month 1	Month 2	Month 3	Month 4	Month 5	Month 6	Month 7	Month 8	Month 9	Month 10	Month 11	Month 12
Total Net Sales												
Cost of Sales												
GROSS PROFIT												
Controllable Expenses Salaries												
Payroll taxes												
Security												
Advertising												
Automobile												
Dues and subscriptions												
Legal and accounting												
Office supplies												
Telephone												
Utilities												
Miscellaneous												
Total Controllable Expenses												
Fixed Expenses Depreciation												
Insurance												
Rent												
Taxes and licenses												
Loan payments												
Total Fixed Expenses												
TOTAL EXPENSES												
NET PROFIT (LOSS) (before taxes)												

CASH FLOW PROJECTIONS

A cash flow projection is a forecast of the cash (checks or money orders) a business anticipates receiving and disbursing during the course of a month. Well managed, the cash flow should be sufficient to meet the cash requirements for the following month.

CASH FLOW PROJECTIONS

	Start-up or prior to loan	Month 1	Month 2	Month 3	Month 4	Month 5	Month 6	Month 7	Month 8	Month 9	Month 10	Month 11	Month 12	TOTAL
Cash (beginning of month) Cash on hand														
Cash in bank														
Cash in investments														
Total Cash														
Income (during month) Cash sales														
Credit sales payments														
Investment income														
Loans														
Other cash income														
Total Income														
TOTAL CASH AND INCOME														
Expenses (during month) Inventory or new material														
Wages (including owner's)														
Taxes														
Equipment expense														
Overhead														
Selling expense														
Transportation														
Loan repayment														
Other cash expenses														
TOTAL EXPENSES														
CASH FLOW EXCESS (end of month)														
CASH FLOW CUMULATIVE (monthly)														

Appendix C

Lewis & Renn Associates, Inc.

Business Plan by

STATEMENT OF PURPOSE

EXECUTIVE FASHIONS proposes to lease building space from Sunrise Mall in order to operate its working women's apparel business. An owner's investment of $30,000 and a $10,000 loan will be sufficient to finance rental space, furnishings, and inventory necessary to start a successful and profitable business.

TABLE OF CONTENTS

I. THE BUSINESS

    A.   Description of Business   i

    B.   The Market   i

    C.   The Competition   i

    D.   Location of Business   ii

    E.   Management   ii

    F.   Personnel   ii

    G.   Application and Expected Effect of Investment   iii

    H.   Summary   iii

II. FINANCIAL DATA

    A.   Balance Sheet   iv

    B.   Break-even Analysis   v

    C.   Income Statement

    D.   Cash Flow

    E.   Deviation Analysis

III. SUPPORTING DOCUMENTS

    A.   Resume of Sara Lewis   vi

    B.   Notes   vii

    C.   Appendix   viii

I. THE BUSINESS

A. Description of Business

EXECUTIVE FASHIONS is primarily a merchandising business which specializes in high-quality fashions for the working woman. **EXECUTIVE FASHIONS** also provides wardrobe coordination as well as precoordinated wardrobe kits. We will be open for business September, 1984 and will be open six days a week (Monday-Saturday) from 10 a.m. to 9 p.m.

The retail demand is year-round and steadily growing because of the increasing number of women in the work force.

B. The Market

EXECUTIVE FASHIONS caters primarily to working women in the Oscoda County area. As of 1981, half of all women were part of the work force and the number is even higher today. We expect that the number will continue to increase and as a result, **EXECUTIVE FASHIONS** has much potential for continued growth.

Customers will be attracted by (1) local newspaper and radio advertisements (2) wardrobe coordination demonstrations and (3) our convenient location in the Sunrise Mall.

C. The Competition

EXECUTIVE FASHIONS faces three main types of competition:

(1) Department Stores: large selection in women's clothing but little or no specialization in career fashions. We anticipate department stores to be our major competitors.

(2) Small Retail Clothing Shops: independent and chain clothing merchandisers with little or no specialization in career fashions.

(3) Discount and Low-Quality Clothing Stores: lower-quality clothing at lower prices.

As of yet, there are no specialty clothing stores for working women in the Mio area other than **EXECUTIVE FASHIONS** that provide wardrobe coordination and precoordinated kits.

i

D. Location of Business

EXECUTIVE FASHIONS proposes to lease a one-story building space in the Sunrise Mall, 591 Washington Avenue, located in downtown Mio across from a well-established hotel. The Sunrise Mall is a commercial shopping center and attracts everyday shoppers as well as business people and hotel guests. The building space is divided into: (1) office space; (2) sales counter; (3) sales floor; and (4) storage.

E. Management

Mrs. Sara Lewis, an ex-housewife and mother, will manage EXECUTIVE FASHIONS. Mrs. Lewis has lived in Mio all of her life and obtained her Associates Degree in Business Administration in 1980.

Ms. Carolyn Renn, who worked for eight years as a fashion merchandiser in New York, will co-manage EXECUTIVE FASHIONS and will act as fashion merchandiser for the new business. Ms. Renn is unmarried and lives in Mio.

With Mrs. Lewis's entrepreneurial abilities and Ms. Renn's experience in fashion merchandising, both women believe that they can make EXECUTIVE FASHIONS a successful and unique business. Both will share the responsibilities of coordinating wardrobes, assembling kits, and giving demonstrations.

Salaries will be approximately $800/month but will depend on the success of the new business. Mrs. Lewis is supported by her husband and Ms. Renn is single and has relatively low living expenses.

Mrs. Lewis has employed Mr. Greg Balance, CPA; Mr. Irving Right, lawyer; and Mr. B. Safe, insurance broker. Also, Mrs. Lewis has consulted with other resources, including the GMI Business & Industry Development (BID) Center and the Small Business Assistance (SMA) Center.

F. Personnel

EXECUTIVE FASHIONS will employ one full-time saleswoman upon opening and will hire additional saleswomen as needed. They will initially be paid minimum wage.

G. Application and Expected Effect of Investment

Inventory	$25,000
Furnishing	8,000
Lease of building space for one year	5,000
Reserve	2,000
TOTAL	$40,000

Inventory will consist of an entire line of career fashions for women in various sizes.

Furnishings will include a cash register, display racks, lights, carpeting, and storage shelves.

H. Summary

EXECUTIVE FASHIONS is a start-up business located at 591 Washington Avenue which sells apparel strictly for working women. We also provide wardrobe coordination and consultation as well as precoordinated wardrobe kits. The owner, Mrs. Lewis, is seeking a loan of $10,000 and will invest $30,000 in the business, which will be sufficient to finance rental space, furnishings, and inventory.

Mrs. Lewis will combine her management skills with Ms. Renn's experience in the fashion industry to establish a successful business.

II. FINANCIAL DATA

A. Balance Sheet

EXECUTIVE FASHIONS
Balance Sheet
September 25, 1984

ASSETS

CURRENT ASSETS		
Cash	$ 1,000	
Accounts Receivable	3,000	
Merchandise Inventory	25,000	
FIXED ASSETS		
Real Estate	5,000	
Equipment	8,000	
LESS: Accumulated Depreciation	0	
TOTAL ASSETS		$42,000

LIABILITIES

CURRENT LIABILITIES		
Accounts Payable	7,000	
Unpaid Taxes	5,000	
LONG-TERM LIABILITIES		
Mortgages on Real Estate	4,000	
Notes Payable	11,000	
Bank Loan Payable	10,000	
TOTAL LIABILITIES		37,000
Net Worth		5,000
TOTAL LIABILITIES AND NET WORTH		$42,000

B.   Break-even Analysis

EXECUTIVE FASHIONS

Break-Even Analysis for One Year

Fixed Costs (FC) = $30,000

Variable Costs (VC) = $21,000

Break-even level of sales in dollars (S) = FC + VC

S = $30,000 + $21,000

S = 51,000 = Break-even (where Total Revenue = Total Cost)

C.   INCOME STATEMENT

EXECUTIVE FASHIONS
Income Statement
September 18, 1984 - September 17, 1987

	YEAR I	YEAR II	YEAR III
NET SALES	$60,000	$66,000	$72,600
LESS - COST OF GOODS SOLD	25,000	27,500	30,250
GROSS MARGIN	$35,000	$38,500	$42,350
OPERATING EXPENSES:			
Salaries	$19,200	$21,120	$23,232
Payroll Taxes and Benefits	1,000	1,100	1,210
Rent	5,000	5,500	6,050
Utilities	1,000	1,100	1,210
Office Supplies	150	165	182
Insurance	800	880	968
Advertising	1,000	1,100	1,210
Professional	1,500	1,650	1,815
Miscellaneous	350	385	423
TOTAL OPERATING EXPENSES	$30,000	$33,000	$36,300
OTHER EXPENSE - Loan Interest (12%)	1,200	984	742
TOTAL: ALL EXPENSES	$31,200	$33,984	$37,042
PROFIT (PRETAX)	$ 3,800	$ 4,516	$ 5,308
TAXES	600	700	800
NET PROFIT	$ 3,200	$ 3,816	$ 4,508

vi

D.   CASH FLOW

EXECUTIVE FASHIONS
Cash Flow
October 1984

CASH RECEIPTS - Income from Sales	<u>$5,000</u>
CASH DISBURSEMENTS:	
Cost of Goods	$2,000
Variable Labor	100
Professional	100
Advertising	200
Fixed Cash Disbursements	2,400
Bank Loan	<u>300</u>
TOTAL CASH DISBURSEMENTS	<u>$5,100</u>
NET CASH FLOW	$ (100)
CUMULATIVE CASH FLOW	$ (100)

III. SUPPORTING DOCUMENTS

RESUME OF SARA LEWIS

Office: Home:

951 Washington Avenue   123 Route 6
Mio, MI 48647   Mio, MI 48502
517-826-6000   517-826-5000

BUSINESS EXPERIENCE

<u>Housewife</u>
Raised three children, in charge of household responsibilities.

<u>Smith & Jones</u>
Secretary and Assistant to Mr. James Smith, CPA.

EDUCATION

Associates Degree in Business Administration, Kirtland Community College.

PERSONAL

Married, three children, age 47, member of Church Parish Council.

NOTES

Appendix D

INSURANCE CHECKLIST

TYPE OF INSURANCE	PURCHASE	DO NOT PURCHASE
PROPERTY INSURANCE:		
Fire		
Windstorm		
Hail		
Smoke		
Explosion		
Vandalism		
Water Damage		
Glass		
LIABILITY INSURANCE		
WORKERS' COMPENSATION		
BUSINESS INTERRUPTION		
DISHONESTY:		
Fidelity		
Robbery		
Burglary		
Comprehensive		
PERSONAL:		
Health		
Life		
Key Personnel		

Lewis & Renn Associates
3325 Parkway Drive
Bay City, Michigan 48706
(517) 684-1184

Business Plans Available To Order

How To Start and Manage:

ISBN 0-9628759-3-7 AN APPAREL STORE BUSINESS
ISBN 0-9628759-4-5 A WORD PROCESSING BUSINESS
ISBN 0-9628759-5-3 A GARDEN CENTER BUSINESS
ISBN 0-9628759-6-1 A HAIRSTYLING SHOP BUSINESS
ISBN 0-9628759-7-X A BICYCLE SHOP BUSINESS
ISBN 0-9628759-8-8 A TRAVEL AGENCY BUSINESS
ISBN 0-9628759-9-6 AN ANSWERING SERVICE BUSINESS
ISBN 1-887005-00-5 A HEALTH SPA BUSINESS
ISBN 1-887005-01-3 A RESTAURANT BUSINESS
ISBN 1-887005-02-1 A SPECIALTY FOOD STORE BUSINESS
ISBN 1-887005-03-X A WELDING BUSINESS
ISBN 1-887005-04-8 A DAY CARE CENTER BUSINESS
ISBN 1-887005-05-6 A FLOWER & PLANT STORE BUSINESS
ISBN 1-887005-06-4 A CONSTRUCTION ELECTRICIAN BUSINESS
ISBN 1-887005-07-2 A HOUSECLEANING SERVICE BUSINESS
ISBN 1-887005-08-0 A NURSING SERVICE BUSINESS
ISBN 1-887005-09-9 A BOOKKEEPING SERVICE BUSINESS
ISBN 1-887005-10-2 A SECRETARIAL SERVICE BUSINESS
ISBN 1-887005-11-0 A HOME-BASED BUSINESS
ISBN 1-887005-12-9 A BED & BREAKFAST BUSINESS
ISBN 1-887005-13-7 AN ENERGY SPECIALIST BUSINESS
ISBN 1-887005-14-5 A GUARD SERVICE BUSINESS
ISBN 1-887005-15-3 A SOFTWARE DESIGN BUSINESS
ISBN 1-887005-16-1 AN AIR CONDITIONING-HEATING BUSINESS
ISBN 1-887005-20-X A PLUMBING SERVICE BUSINESS
ISBN 1-887005-21-8 A SEWING SERVICE BUSINESS
ISBN 1-887005-22-6 A CARPENTRY SERVICE BUSINESS
ISBN 1-887005-23-4 A HOME ATTENDANT SERVICE BUSINESS
ISBN 1-887005-24-2 A TREE SERVICE BUSINESS
ISBN 1-887005-25-0 A DAIRY FARMING BUSINESS
ISBN 1-887005-26-9 A FARM EQUIPMENT REPAIR SERVICE BUSINESS
ISBN 1-887005-27-7 A CHILDREN'S CLOTHING STORE BUSINESS
ISBN 1-887005-28-5 A WOMEN'S APPAREL STORE BUSINESS
ISBN 1-887005-29-3 A CONVENIENCE FOOD STORE BUSINESS
ISBN 1-887005-30-7 A PEST CONTROL SERVICE BUSINESS

How To:

ISBN 1-887005-17-X WRITE A SUCCESSFUL BUSINESS PLAN
ISBN 1-887005-18-8 MARKET YOUR BUSINESS FOR THE 21ST CENTURY
ISBN 1-887005-19-6 FINANCE YOUR BUSINESS FOR THE 21ST CENTURY

Lewis & Renn Associates
3325 Parkway Drive
Bay City, Michigan 48706
(517) 684-1184

Business Plans Available To Order

How To Start and Manage:

ISBN 1-887005-31-5 A PRINTING BUSINESS
ISBN 1-887005-32-3 AN ICE CREAM BUSINESS
ISBN 1-887005-33-1 A MAIL ORDER BUSINESS
ISBN 1-887005-34-X A BOOKSTORE BUSINESS
ISBN 1-887005-35-8 A HOME FURNISHINGS BUSINESS
ISBN 1-887005-36-6 A RETAIL FLORIST BUSINESS
ISBN 1-887005-37-4 A RADIO-TELEVISION REPAIR SHOP BUSINESS
ISBN 1-887005-38-2 A DRYCLEANING BUSINESS
ISBN 1-887005-39-0 A HARDWARE STORE BUSINESS
ISBN 1-887005-40-4 A MARINE RETAILING BUSINESS
ISBN 1-887005-41-2 AN OFFICE PRODUCTS BUSINESS
ISBN 1-887005-42-0 A PHARMACY BUSINESS
ISBN 1-887005-43-9 A FISH FARMING BUSINESS
ISBN 1-887005-44-7 A PERSONNEL REFERRAL SERVICE BUSINESS
ISBN 1-887005-45-5 A SOLAR ENERGY BUSINESS
ISBN 1-887005-46-3 A BUILDING SERVICE CONTRACTING BUSINESS
ISBN 1-887005-47-1 A RETAIL DECORATING PRODUCTS BUSINESS
ISBN 1-887005-48-X A SPORTING GOODS STORE BUSINESS
ISBN 1-887005-49-8 A RETAIL GROCERY STORE BUSINESS
ISBN 1-887005-50-1 A COSMETOLOGY BUSINESS
ISBN 1-887005-51-X A FRANCHISED BUSINESS
ISBN 1-887005-52-8 AN ELECTRONICS INDUSTRY CONSULTING PRACTICE BUSINESS
ISBN 1-887005-53-6 AN INDEPENDENT CONSULTING PRACTICE BUSINESS
ISBN 1-887005-54-4 AN INDEPENDENT TRUCKING BUSINESS
ISBN 1-887005-55-2 AN ACCOUNTING SERVICE BUSINESS
ISBN 1-887005-56-0 A NURSERY BUSINESS

TO ORDER BUSINESS PLANS

Please Remit To:

LEWIS AND RENN ASSOCIATES
10315 HARMONY DRIVE
INTERLOCHEN, MICHIGAN 49643

Business Guide # _____ Title _____
Business Guide # _____ Title _____

Name _____   Business Guide _____
Address _____   Plus 4% Sales Tax _____
City _____   U.S. Shipping & Postage ___$1.00___
State _____ Zip _____   Total _____

$9.95 EACH + $3.00 POSTAGE & HANDLING

INDEX

A

Analyze 1
Achieving 9
Assemble financial data 9
Activities 11
Accumulated profits 25
Authority 57
Application software 32
Accessories 90

B

Business plan 9
Budgeted balance sheet 10
Brochure 20
Business startups 34
Benchmark 42
Balance sheet 54

C

Critical sector 2
Complexity 9
Categories 11
Customers 12
Customer profile 16
Clientele 19
Cash flow 31
Computerized 50

D

Dynamic 2
Desist 7
Degree of complexity 9
Demographics 12
Delineate 13
Duplicate 20
Documentation 83
Data safety 88

E

Exciting challenges 1
Employer identification number 7
Energies 11
Electronic gear 53
Expendability 87

F

Financial planning 10
Financial health 24
Fidelity bonds 39
Franchising 60

G

Goals 21
Goodwill 25
Group health 39
Graphically 48

H

Home-based business 1
Homework 33
Hardware 84

I

Income generator 1
Internal revenue service 7
Identify 11
Interpretation 25

J

Jurisdictions 7
Just as important 24
Job experience 35

K

Keep track of expenses 24
Key code items 38
Key subsidiary documents 43
Keymen 58

L

License 7
Location 10
Leasehold improvements 26

M

Managerial skills 1
Marketing strategy 9
Measurable financial objectives 9
Marginally 45

Mail order 47
Minicomputer 80
Microcomputer 80
Minimize 89

N
Necessary 11
Nonpersonal 20
Net income 25
Net worth 26
Nightmare 36
Niche 44

O
Objective analysis 9
Office of taxation 8
Organizational plan 9
Opportunities 12
Overview 14

P
Payroll report 8
Planning process 10
Productivity 12
Portray 15
Pro-forma 51
Processor 85

Q
Question 20
Quality of systems software 86

R
Rewarding experience 2
Restrictions 7
Registration requirements 7
Realistic plan 9

S
Stamina 2
Startup costs 6
Social security tax 8
Scope 11
Spectrum 33
Stable 46
Sources of funds 52

T
Technological innovations 6
Transform 9
Target market 10
Tool of financial management 25

U
Unemployment tax 8
Use tax 8
Unit sales 18
Unprofitable merchandise 24
Untrained entrepreneurs 33
Unemotionable look 42
Ultimately 46

V
Various 22
Variety 23
Vital information 36
Vendors 39
Volunteer 47
Venture 65

W
Work-experience 6
Work certificate 7
Wage tax statement 8
What to advertise 20
Weekly newspaper 22
Worksheet 29

Y
Your business 20
Yearly operations 24

Z
Zoning board 7
Zoned editions 22